:ers

James L. Armentrout

CHRIST IN YOUR MARRIAGE

Augsburg Fortress

Minneapolis

CHRIST IN YOUR MARRIAGE
Worship for Life

Copyright © 2007 Augsburg Fortress. All rights reserved. Except for brief quotations in critical articles or reviews, no part of this book may be reproduced in any manner without prior written permission from the publisher. Write to: Permissions, Augsburg Fortress, Box 1209, Minneapolis, MN 55440.

All Scripture quotations are from New Revised Standard Version Bible, copyright © 1989 Division of Christian Education of the National Council of the Churches of Christ in the United States of America. All rights reserved. Used by permission.

Quotations marked *Evangelical Lutheran Worship* are reprinted from *Evangelical Lutheran Worship*, copyright © 2006 Evangelical Lutheran Church in America, admin. Augsburg Fortress.

Editor: Suzanne Burke
Cover design: Laurie Ingram
Text design: James Satter

ISBN 978-0-8006-2114-8

The paper used in this publication meets the minimum requirements of American National Standard for Information Sciences—Permanence of Paper for Printed Library Materials, ANSI Z329.48-1984.

Manufactured in the U.S.A.

11   10   09   08   07   1   2   3   4   5   6   7   8   9   10

Contents

Acknowledgments

We give thanks to God for the privilege of working together and writing this book. We give thanks to God for our wives, Jennifer and Brandy. By your love and commitment to marriage you have taught us more than you can possibly imagine. We give thanks for our children, Eric and Benjamin, Nicholas, Nathan, and Joshua. Even before any of you spoke a single word you taught us of the importance of marriage, and renewed our commitments to our beautiful wives. Thanks be to God.

We give thanks to God for our parents, Lewin and Norma, Clare and Jan, who modeled loving commitments to God, to marriage, to the church, and to one another and gave us both solid foundations in our lives of faith.

We give thanks to God for Martin Saarinen, pastor and mentor. He has modeled faithful service to Christ within the covenant of marriage and the church. Without knowing it, he planted the seeds for this book.

We give thanks to God for Cheryl Dieter, Renewing Worship Project Coordinator, for her encouragement and support of this project. We give thanks to God for our editor Suzanne Burke. Her insightful guidance through the editing process greatly improved this work. Finally, we could not have written this without the *Evangelical Lutheran Worship* marriage rite. This faithful resource provided a deep and meaningful inspiration. More significantly, it deepened our understanding of Christian marriage generally and our marriages specifically.

Introduction

You hold in your hands an invitation and an opportunity. This book invites you to be intentional about your relationship with your spouse-to-be, and with Jesus. Take the time to read these reflections together. The questions at the conclusion of each chapter are opportunities for you both to share more of who you are as human beings and as children of God.

This book is suitable for use as part of premarital counseling with a pastor. At the same time it could be used by a couple without additional guidance. Several chapters used together might also be used as part of a group event involving many couples preparing for marriage. No matter how you use this resource, the reflections and questions will help you discover more about this person you love, who you are soon to marry, and about Jesus who loves you.

The first half of the book is intended to be used in the months leading up to your marriage. You might choose to read these once a week for a number of months. You may prefer to read them more frequently. Those details are for you to sort out.

The second half of the book consists of twelve devotions, one for each month during your first year of marriage. In the excitement over the day of their wedding, couples often forget to plan for the many, many days of marriage that will follow. You are invited to spend time during your first year of marriage to remember the words spoken to you and by you on your wedding day. You might discover these words have new and deeper meaning as the months go by.

In case you are wondering, the chapters in Part Two *are* in the correct order. The choice to begin at the end and end at the beginning is intentional. This order is intended to remind you that marriage is not linear, from start to finish, but cyclical. Each day as you wake your marriage begins anew, with challenges and joys, celebrations and heartaches. Each day you rise, by the grace of God a forgiven sinner, with another opportunity to live out your marriage vows. Thanks be to God.

Clearly, a strength of the marriage service in *Evangelical Lutheran Worship* is the variety of options within the rite itself. Rather than reflect on every option, we chose to focus each chapter on one of the options. If a particular devotion focuses on an option different from the one you selected for your marriage service, you might choose to spend time talking about the differences and the merits of each option. Any time spent reflecting on the words prayed over you at your wedding will bless you.

As you use this book, enjoy the reflections and questions and one another. May your life together, your love for one another, and your love for Jesus be strengthened through this book, by the grace of God.

Part One

Devotions As You Prepare for Marriage

Chapter 1

In the Beginning: Baptism

So you are going to get married. The big day is right around the corner. You have many details to consider and issues to resolve, all in the midst of swirling emotions. It is a time of excitement and fear, anticipation and trepidation. You probably want time to speed up and slow down all at once. Today we are going to slow down. We are going to travel back in time to when it all began with you two, but not "you two" as in the two of you as a couple. In this case the beginning refers to your grounding, your foundation. Today we are going to consider your relationship with God.

Probably before you even thought about this marriage, perhaps before the two of you met, maybe before you ever stopped to consider the opposite sex, God laid claim on your life forever. Maybe people who loved you brought you to the baptismal font or as an adult you followed the Holy Spirit's lead to baptism. Regardless, it was there, before the gathered people of God, that your life was changed forever. Water and words combined, and it was done. Then the pastor said to you, "Child of God, you have been sealed by the Holy Spirit and marked with the cross of Christ forever." That moment was the public confirmation of the claim God placed on your life in the womb. In the words of the prophet Jeremiah, "Before I formed you in the womb I knew you" (Jer. 1:5). Even then you were precious to God.

Thus began your life's holy calling to serve the creator of all that is, seen and unseen, known and unknown, with every moment of your existence. Holy callings are not reserved for those called pastors or those who work in the church in some formal capacity. All baptized Christians are called by God to serve in the world. Some, to be certain, are called to serve as pastors. Most, however, are called to serve in other ways using other gifts. Many times we serve God by volunteering through the church. You may prepare a meal at a homeless shelter or swing a hammer at a Habitat for Humanity house. Certainly these are important ways in which we can be faithful servants of our God. Jesus said in Matthew 25:40, "Truly I tell you, just as you did it to one of the least of these who are members of my family, you did it to me." Service to the community around us is a holy calling but it is not the only way we serve God.

From the moment of your baptism you have grown in faith as a part of a community of believers. If you were baptized in a Lutheran congregation, you may have been welcomed by the church formally when, in unison, the congregation said these or similar words: "We welcome you into the Lord's family. We receive you as fellow members of the body of Christ, children of the same heavenly Father, and workers with us in the kingdom of God." Some form of this welcome exists in the baptismal rite of many traditions. So it isn't just you who serve, but we who serve our Lord together. We serve God by worshiping together as the people of God. We serve God by caring for home and family. We serve God by respecting and caring for parents and other relatives. Because even life itself is given to us by God, every moment of our lives is spent in the service of God.

Your upcoming life as a husband or a wife will provide daily opportunities to serve God. Caring for your spouse, respecting him, listening to her, bearing one another's burdens, sharing all the joys and sorrows of life together: All these and more are opportunities for serving God. The work that you do with this book leading up to your marriage is not done simply for yourselves, so that you can have a better, healthier, more loving marriage. We pray you are blessed with all that and more, but this work is done so that your life together might glorify God. We pray that your mutual respect, love, adoration, and all the rest might, in some small way, reflect the love of God we have come to know through Christ Jesus our Lord. Your marriage will be a continuation of the journey that began with your baptism. As you grow together in your marriage may you also grow in faith, love, and obedience to the will of God.

Questions for conversation

1. Share the story of your baptism. Where was it? Who presided? Who was there? Who are your godparents or sponsors?

2. What is one way you have lived out your baptismal calling?

Chapter 2

A Holy Hello: Greeting

The grace of our Lord Jesus Christ, the love of God, and the communion of the Holy Spirit be with you all.

Have you ever said, "Good morning, how are you?" to someone who actually wanted to tell you how they felt? How wonderful to spend the next five minutes hearing about the dog who relieved himself on the carpet again, the hassles with the kids, or some graphic medical procedure. The truth is most of the time when we ask someone, "How are you doing?" the last thing in the world we want to know is how they are doing. We are exchanging pleasantries, formalities, expected words of greeting and nothing more.

One call-in radio host actually hangs up on anyone who begins his or her comments by asking, "How are you doing?" Why? Because, he will say, "I do not want to know how you are doing and you don't really care about me. Just get to your point and be interesting." Most of us would not be so crass, but few people treat these exchanges as anything other than polite moments before the real conversation begins.

In the church life is different. We do not begin with "Good morning, how are you?" We begin instead with a greeting from 2 Corinthians 13:13: "The grace of our Lord Jesus Christ, the love of God, and the communion of the Holy Spirit be with you all." The first words of your wedding service will not be empty formalities, but a holy greeting to you and all those gathered. They are not words you hear every day walking down the street. They signal to all those gathered that we are beginning something different and significant.

Worship is beginning—a worship service planned around the occasion of your wedding, but still a worship service. The focus of the service is not your wedding, but worship and praise of God, the foundation of your marriage. Your marriage is an opportunity to praise and glorify God. Your life together, at its best, is a reflection of the relationship between God and all creation.

This relationship is described in the words of greeting that begin worship. Indeed, these words of greeting serve as an appetizer for the feast of worship to come. In the course of worship we discover the grace of Jesus flowing over us and washing us from head to toe. From the experience of Jesus we come to know the love of God the Father. It brings us together, one with another through the work of the Holy Spirit.

Jesus the Son is the one who introduces us to God the Father: "No one knows the Son except the Father, and no one knows the Father except the Son and anyone to whom the Son chooses to reveal him" (Matt. 11:27). We meet this Jesus forgiving those cast aside, like the lepers and tax collectors. We meet this Jesus generously feeding vast multitudes of people. We meet this Jesus as he dies on the cross for the life of all people. There we see the ultimate vision of grace, and a glimpse of the depth of God's love for humanity.

The love of God is most closely associated with forgiving. It is a powerful yet weak, forgiving love. It is the only type of love that makes relationships possible. Without forgiveness, all relationships are doomed to fail, for over time we all sin against one another. It will be true for your marriage, even as it has been true for every other marriage.

God calls us to forgive as we have first been forgiven. We meet this difficult challenge through the presence of the Holy Spirit. It is this Spirit of peace, gentleness, and mercy that works in and through human relationships making our lives together possible.

In the days and weeks and even years to come, you will face challenges as a couple. Indeed, from this day forth you face nothing alone, for anything that happens to one of you affects the other as well. Every step of the way you are in it together and God is with you as well. No matter what you do or who you are, the Holy Spirit will be with you, nudging you, pulling you, and leading you to faithfulness and the forgiveness that makes marriages strong.

The path before you is wonderful, exciting, hope-filled, and beautiful. At the same time challenges lurk ahead. Ancient map makers, when describing dangerous or unknown territories, were known to write "Here there be tigers" on their maps as a word of warning and caution. Maybe these words should be written on your marriage license, too! Tigers crouch, waiting for you. You may face unknown territories called in-laws and children. Even dangers, such as credit cards and debt, may lie ahead.

These challenges can be overwhelming at times. For this reason, your wedding service begins with a reminder of the commitment God has made to you and your marriage. In the years to come you will discover that when tigers lurk in the bushes, "the grace of our Lord Jesus Christ, the love of God, and the communion of the Holy Spirit" will sustain you in your journey, bring you together through forgiveness, and give you hope for the future. Thanks be to God.

Questions for conversation

1. What might be some of the tigers in your future?
2. Describe a time you forgave someone as God has forgiven you. What happened? How did it feel? How did things turn out?

Chapter 3

A Faithful Focus: Introduction (Part One)

"Attention! May I have your attention please?" A voice can be heard over the public address system in the crowded room. "I have something I'd like to say…"

or

Ding, ding, ding, ding. The high-pitched ring of the crystal champagne flute echoes across the banquet hall. The best man is gently tapping the flute with his fork. The room begins to fall silent. The guests have heard this sound before. They know what it means. They direct their attention to the head table and wait for the best man's speech.

or

Dear friends: We have come together in the presence of God to witness the marriage of *name* and *name*, to surround them with our prayers, and to share in their joy. (*Evangelical Lutheran Worship* Leaders Edition, p. 676)

How do you get a room full of people focused on what is about to happen? How do you get everyone on the same page? More importantly, how do you help them focus on what their role and responsibility is in the activity at hand?

The people at your wedding will come from all walks of life. The quality and character of their relationships with each of you will be different. The quality and character of their relationships with God will also be different. Differences will be present regardless of the number of people attending your wedding.

Maybe, at your mother's behest, you will invite her coworker who still can't remember that it is you and not your sibling being married. You may choose to keep your wedding small and intimate, just immediate family. Those who are gathered—the assembly—may not all be Christian. Still, your guests will be gathering with you for a specific reason in a specific setting and context.

In the midst of all this diversity, large assembly or small, the introduction to the marriage service identifies those gathered as "friends." In doing so, a broader sense of community is created, strengthening the assembly's relationships with one another.

More than that, though, the diversity of people involved in your wedding won't be limited to the gathered assembly. St. Paul writes in 1 Corinthians 12:12-13, "For just as the body is one and has many members, and all the members of the body, though many, are one body, so it is with Christ. For in the one Spirit we were all baptized into one body—Jews or Greeks, slaves or free—and we were all made to drink of one Spirit." By virtue of your baptism, you will also be joined by the whole church of every time and place. So the support you will receive in your marriage will come from millions upon millions of brothers and sisters in Christ. You will be supported in a much broader, richer, and deeper way than you probably realized.

The introduction also calls the assembly to action. Your guests will do more than observe and their wedding-related activity will consist of more than buying a gift from the registry. They will be active participants in your wedding service. They will pray for your faithfulness to God and to one another in your life together.

Being a great organizer is one of God's specialties. God has been well known for gathering up a diverse group of people and focusing them in just this way.

> Hear, O Israel: The LORD is our God, the LORD alone. You shall love the LORD your God with all your heart, and with all your soul, and with all your might. (Deut. 6:4-5)

In this passage, Israel is reminded they are God's people and as such they, like those at your wedding, are called into action. When your guests gather for your wedding, in all of their diversity, they will celebrate with you the gift of Christ and the way in which your life together may be a reflection of his love for the world.

Questions for conversation

1. Who are the people, the friends, you will be inviting to your wedding?

2. How do they already support your relationship in a Christ-like way?

Chapter 4

A Gracious Gift:
Introduction (Part Two)

What do you love the most? What is your most prized possession? The wristwatch I (Paul) wear does not always keep the best time. Some days it is accurate, but if I don't wear it for a day it can be as much as 15 minutes slow. The date counts to 31, so for the months that have fewer days I have to adjust it by hand. But this watch is dear to me and I love wearing it. You see, it was a gift from my great uncle who wore it for many years before I got it. It is not perfect, not as sleek or efficient as a watch you might find in the store today, but I never want to replace it. Whenever I check the time it reminds me of my uncle, and those memories are precious to me.

What does this have to do with your marriage? Consider these words from the *Evangelical Lutheran Worship* marriage rite, spoken by the minister to introduce the service:

> The scriptures teach us that the bond and covenant of marriage is a gift of God in which a man and a woman are joined as one, an image of the union of Christ and the church. As _name_ and _name_ make their promises to each other today, we remember that at Cana in Galilee our Lord Jesus Christ made the wedding feast a sign of God's reign of love. (*Evangelical Lutheran Worship* Leaders Edition, p. 676)

These words remind us marriage is precious in part because it comes to us as a gift from God. Your marriage does not belong to you. It is not a possession you own; it is a gift from God. It is precious in large part because of the giver of the gift. Marriage, as a gift from a loving God, means you can trust that in your marriage you are never alone. You are never just husband and wife, disconnected from the people and world around you. God the Father, with the Son, through the Holy Spirit, is always with you, caring for you, and sustaining you in your life together.

God's loving presence is why we can celebrate so joyfully at a wedding. You are beginning a new part of your life. Things will change for you. Once you have seen one another in awkward and embarrassing times, you will never be the same. Once you have seen one another first thing in the morning with gravity-defying hair, smelled the morning breath, and noticed the line of drool running down a pristine cheek, your relationship has changed forever. Once you see one another as you truly are, true love has a place to grow. It is the process of two becoming one flesh, loving one another with all your beauty and all your flaws. In some small way your relationship, your love for one another, comes to resemble the love that Jesus Christ has for the church.

We celebrate this gift of God. Jesus himself knew the importance of celebrating gifts from God. When the wine gave out at the wedding at Cana in Galilee, he provided more as a gift of grace (John 2:1-11). But grace from God can be an overwhelming thing. Jesus did not give a few bottles of wine. He made wine by the vat. He gave hundreds of gallons of wine—more wine than anyone had ever seen in one place at any other time. All that wine is a sign, a reminder of the grace of God, which will sustain you in your marriage.

One more thing needs to be said before moving forward into the rest of the marriage service. The minister may use these or similar words:

> Let us enter into this celebration confident that, through the Holy Spirit, Christ is present with us now also. We pray that this couple may fulfill God's purpose for the whole of their lives.

As Christians we are confident in God's promise that, no matter where we go or what we do, God in Christ Jesus is present with us. With Jesus beside you, in, with, and under you and your marriage, you can move forward together, trusting God's promise.

You do not go alone, and you are never abandoned, so that you may live godly lives until the day of Jesus Christ.

Questions for conversation

1. Share with each other the greatest gift you bring to your marriage.

2. What is your fiancé's most precious gift to you?

Chapter 5

Promises, Promises:
Declaration of Intention

Do you ever feel all alone? Do you ever feel as though no one cares? Sometimes when life gets hard we think we are all alone, isolated and cut off. We think that it is up to us and us alone to deal with whatever faces us. On your wedding day you will stand before your guests with all eyes turned toward you, and it just might seem like you are all alone.

Read through the following declaration of intention from the *Evangelical Lutheran Worship* marriage rite. Consider the list of expectations. Consider what you are committing yourself to.

> <u>Name</u>, living in the promise of God,
> [joined to Christ in baptism,]
> will you give yourself to <u>name</u> in love and faithfulness?
> Will you share your life with *her/him*,
> in joy and in sorrow, in health and in sickness,
> for richer, for poorer, for better, for worse,
> and will you be faithful to *her/him* as long as you both shall live?
> *Response:* I will.
> (*Evangelical Lutheran Worship* Leaders Edition, p. 677)

With all eyes on you, that "I will" may not come out as strongly and confidently as you might like. These promises are huge and not a short-term commitment. "As long as you both shall live" is about as long as it gets.

The good news is that you are not alone in this undertaking. The promise of our Lord Jesus Christ is that his holy presence is with you, come what may. Jesus says in Matthew 28:20, "I am with you always, to the end of the age." In addition, your families may be asked to add their blessing to your marriage:

Will you, the families of _name_ and _name_, give your love and blessing to this new family?
The families respond: We will.

And then the entire assembly, all those gathered, become part of your marriage when they respond to the following question:

Will all of you, by God's grace, uphold and care for _name_ and _name_ in their life together?
We will.

The commitment of your families and the whole gathered assembly to support your marriage is one way marriage in the church is radically different from a civil ceremony. Bonded together by the love of Jesus Christ, the entire community pledges its support for your marriage. You are not alone in your joys or your sorrows. A lifelong commitment to faithfulness and fidelity to one another is not an easy undertaking. On days that challenge your relationship there are people to turn to. Your family will pledge their support for you. All those present will pledge their commitment to support your marriage. Look to their love and wisdom.

In the New Testament book of Hebrews, the writer describes countless faithful witnesses to Jesus Christ and then concludes:

Therefore, since we are surrounded by so great a cloud of witnesses, let us also lay aside every weight and the sin that clings so closely, and let us run with perseverance the race that is set before us, looking to Jesus the pioneer and perfecter of our faith, who for the sake of the joy that was set before him endured the cross, disregarding its shame, and has taken his seat at the right hand of the throne of God. (Heb. 12:1-2)

The next time you worship together, look around. In every couple you will discover people who together have endured hardship and pain. You may even see couples who have suffered some of life's greatest losses. They may be parents whose children have died, husbands and wives who deal with alcoholism or abuse. Some couples struggle with the weight of credit card debt or face disease or the possibility of death. Other couples may have difficulty having a conversation. All around you are people who have discovered how to live with one another in love. All around you are couples who have endured and found hope, joy, and love on the other side. These couples are your cloud of witnesses. Together they stand as signs of God's love for humanity, and reminders that the lifelong commitment of fidelity is possible even in this crazy world. You may want to consider sharing a meal with a couple from your church who have been married for decades. As you eat together, look and listen for the strengths of their relationship. Ask for their advice and learn from their experience.

Questions for conversation

1. Whose marriages would you want to model your own marriage after? Why?

2. What are some strengths you see in other marriages? How might your marriage reflect these strengths?

Chapter 6

The Greatest Gift: Prayer of the Day

What are you including in your gift registry? Have you ever thought about identifying prayer as a gift that you would like to receive? It is, after all, one of the best gifts you will receive on your wedding day.

Read this prayer of the day from the *Evangelical Lutheran Worship* marriage service:

> Eternal God, our creator and redeemer, as you gladdened the wedding at Cana in Galilee by the presence of your Son, so bring your joy to this wedding by his presence now. Look in favor upon _name_ and _name_ and grant that they, rejoicing in all your gifts, may at length celebrate the unending marriage feast with Christ our Lord, who lives and reigns with you and the Holy Spirit, one God, now and forever. (*Evangelical Lutheran Worship* Leaders Edition, p. 678)

What makes this prayer such a great gift? You can't spend it. You can't wear it. You can't eat off of it. You can't drink out of it. It's not a request for unlimited wealth, perfect health, or an extra-long honeymoon. So why is it special?

Consider the wedding at Cana (John 2:1-11). Here Jesus attends a wedding at which the wine runs out near the end of the party. To demonstrate who he is, Jesus provides the bridegroom with more wine. The Gospel of John records this event as Jesus' first "sign" or miracle. Part of the unique character of this story, though, is Jesus didn't run down to the corner grocery and pick up a few bottles of the cheap stuff. Jesus created over one hundred gallons of the finest wine.

It was an absurd gesture. A much smaller amount of lower quality wine would have sufficed. In fact, Jesus could have easily gotten away with it. Even the chief steward expected the cheap stuff near the end of the celebration. He said to the bridegroom, "Everyone serves the good wine first and then the inferior wine after the guests have become drunk. But you have kept the good wine until now" (John 2:10). Only the best would do from Jesus. Still, the vast quantity of incredible wine wasn't the truly great gift at the wedding at Cana. The greatest gift was the presence of Christ himself. His presence there provided a foretaste of the great and eternal feast to come.

The gathered assembly, in their support for your marriage, won't just pray for goodness in your marriage. The prayers won't be limited to petitions for happiness and generosity. The prayers won't simply include cries to God for a lasting relationship that mirrors Christ's relationship with the church. Certainly, the assembly will pray for these things, but in the prayer of the day they will pray that you have the best of the best. They will pray for you to have the most precious gift: the presence of Christ Jesus at your wedding and in your marriage.

Through Christ, the bridegroom of the church, the gifts of love and hope, peace and grace will be poured out with great generosity and extravagance, like the wine at the wedding at Cana.

Questions for conversation

1. How do you think your guests would respond if you included "prayer" on your gift registry?

2. What will your prayers be for your fiancé on your wedding day?

3. How is your future spouse a gift to you from God?

Chapter 7

Words of Wisdom: Vows

On your wedding day you will speak some of the most important words of your life. A picture might be worth a thousand words, but on the day of your wedding the small handful of words that are your vows to one another will take on greater significance in your life than almost anything else you have ever spoken.

Even though the world may devalue words, the church has always understood their value and power. In the creation it was the spoken word of God that began it all. "Then God said, 'Let there be light'; and there was light" (Gen. 1:3). God's powerful words did so much. Water and the word combined to baptize you, claiming you forever as a child of God. It is Jesus who is the Word of God in the flesh, living and breathing and living out God's love for humanity. No matter how technologically savvy our culture gets, the church will always rely on words, those small ones we speak to one another and the holy Word who is Jesus himself.

Having understood "mere" words from this perspective, consider the words of your marriage vows. You can choose your vows from among various forms, but the vows you speak should promise unreserved sharing and fidelity until death parts you. You might read the following form of the vows to one another and reflect on them together:

The presiding minister may address the couple in these or similar words.

Name and *name*, I invite you to declare your vows to one another.

The couple may join hands. Each promises faithfulness to the other in these or similar words.

In the presence of God and this community,

I, *name*, take you, *name*, to be my *wife/husband;*

to have and to hold from this day forward,

in joy and in sorrow, in plenty and in want,
in sickness and in health,
to love and to cherish, as long as we both shall live.
This is my solemn vow.

Notice the vows do not provide a list to choose from. This is not a massive salad bar where you pick and choose lettuce, dressings, tomatoes, or even jalapeño slices as you wish. These vows promise you will get everything on the list, with no picking and choosing. You cannot sign up for joy, plenty, and health and go on vacation when sorrow, want, and sickness come to visit.

These words you declare to one another mark the beginning of your married life. From this point forward you will be different, no longer dating, but now husband and wife. Trusting in the words you speak to one another, in the presence of God and the assembly, you have a person with whom you can be open and honest. In this great gift from God, you have found another to share your hopes and dreams. In your spouse you have a person who has committed to share life with you.

You accept each other and all the beauty and frailty that is you. Together you will be supported and strengthened by the love God has for each of you. It is our fervent prayer that as the years go by, your marriage will grow stronger, you will draw ever closer to one another, and your relationship will continue to reflect the holy love of God for all people.

Questions for conversation

1. Describe your thoughts and feelings as you read the vows to one another.

2. What excites you most as you prepare to begin your life together?

3. What are you most anxious about as you prepare to begin your life together?

Chapter 8

Sacred Symbols: Giving of Rings

Symbols point to some reality greater than themselves. Red roses are symbols of love and fidelity. If the flowers are of another variety they might have another message behind them: "Get well," "I miss you," "I'm thinking about you," and so on. Beyond flowers, our lives are surrounded by symbols. The eagle is a symbol of freedom and power both within the Hebrew Scriptures and for many citizens of the United States. The World Trade Center towers in New York City were symbols of American financial power around the world. Corporate logos are powerful symbols. Whenever my (James's) young son Eric sees a sign for the home improvement store Lowe's, he says, "Daddy!" The Lowe's corporate logo doesn't make him think of tools. It makes him think of his daddy.

Wedding rings are also powerful symbols. They are visible signs pointing to the nature of your relationship. They let the world around you know that you have committed yourself to another. You have made a lifelong covenant of fidelity—through good times and bad, in sickness and in health. You have made this commitment in the context of a culture in which the words "new and improved" are two of the most popular words in the advertising industry. This attitude leads us to be on the lookout for the next best thing, even in relationships. In that respect, your rings and the covenant they represent are shocking to the world.

St. Paul wrote about all kinds of behaviors and attitudes that are embraced by the world and should be shunned by his fellow Christian brothers and sisters.

> Live by the Spirit, I say, and do not gratify the desires of the flesh. For what the flesh desires is opposed to the Spirit and what the Spirit desires is opposed to the flesh; for these are opposed to each other, to prevent you from doing what you want ... Now the

works of the flesh are obvious: fornication, impurity, licentious-ness, idolatry, sorcery, enmities, strife, jealousy, anger, quarrels, dissensions, factions, envy, drunkenness, carousing, and things like these. (Gal. 5:16-17, 19-21a)

These behaviors, attitudes, and unhealthy forms of relation-ship are contrary to what God wants for us. Rather than build healthy, strong, vibrant, and faithful relationships between our-selves and God, they destroy relationships. Your wedding rings announce to the world that you have committed yourselves to a way of life standing not just in contrast, but in defiant opposition to the world and its demands.

Your ring is an outward symbol, a tangible sign of your love and fidelity to your partner. This commitment is made clear by the words you speak as you exchange rings: "<u>Name</u>, I give you this ring as a sign of my love and faithfulness." Your rings are visible reminders of the significant commitment you make to one another. Your rings are also a symbol of God's love poured into your mar-riage. It is God who sustains your love when you are weak, angry, hurt, and resentful. In those most difficult times, you will be able to look at your ring and be reminded you are not in this alone, and God is with you both.

Questions for conversation

1. Do you plan to wear wedding rings? Why or why not?
2. What are other symbols of your love and fidelity?
3. As you select the rings that you will give to one another, what kind of rings will you choose? Why?
4. How will your lives be different when you wear a wedding ring?

Chapter 9

Joyous Beginnings: Acclamation

The *acclamation* is an important moment in the marriage service. Read the following words and consider the difference they will make in your life.

> *The presiding minister addresses the assembly.*
> <u>Name</u> and <u>name</u>, by their promises before God and in the presence of this assembly, have joined themselves to one another as husband and wife. Those whom God has joined together let no one separate.
> **Amen. Thanks be to God.**

Now it is official. During the wedding rehearsal you can practice almost every part of the marriage service. Readers can practice reading, ushers can practice getting people to their seats, you can practice saying your vows to one another. But there comes a point when you have to stop, or at least pause, because at that moment in the service you make a shift from being two single people to being husband and wife, officially married.

It is like standing on the Continental Divide and wondering whether the water you pour out from your cup will end in the Pacific or Atlantic Ocean. It is one or the other. Once you were not husband and wife and now you are.

As the day of your wedding approaches it is a growing realization. Consider paying the bill at a restaurant. As an engaged couple, it no longer matters who pays for dinner because the money, for all intents and purposes, is coming from the same place from now on. Any money you spend is no longer just your own to spend as you wish. In a real way you are spending your fiancé's money as well. It does not matter how you choose to divide up bank accounts. You can have separate checking accounts or one you share; either way, all the money coming into the household must be used to pay all of the household's bills.

This new reality in your life as a married person means all the decisions you make have an impact on your spouse's life. You cannot act alone any more. This part of what it means to be married is significant in the new relationship you will soon share.

Marriage will create challenges in all aspects of your life together. How will you decide who will pay the bills? Who is going to clean the bathroom or wash the clothes or cook dinner? All these mundane realities of life will creep into your marriage and one by one they must be discussed and decided.

And then come the big questions of life. The promotion that means so much at work is not something you can simply accept on your own. What are the new responsibilities of the job? Does it require travel away from home or longer hours? How does your spouse feel about those realities? Questions that were relatively easy to answer as a single person become far more challenging as a married person.

With marriage often comes the question of children. Will you have them? When? How many? And then how will you raise them? None of these significant questions are ones either of you can answer alone, for soon you will be married.

During those times that marriage may seem restrictive, confining, and unfair, always remember marriage is a gift from God. The bonds holding you together also give you strength. Your commitment to one another, by the grace of God, is a strength. You do not go into the world alone, but together with your spouse. You have a trusted confidant on whom to rely. You have another who loves and cares for you to trust in for advice and counsel. You have a spouse who will stand together with you through all that is to come. Thanks be to God.

Questions for conversation

1. How are you stronger together than you are alone?

2. What are some wonderful aspects to your new unity?

3. How is this reality a challenge for you?

Chapter 10

A Blessed Relationship:
Marriage Blessing

Can you believe it? You're married! You have declared your vows, exchanged rings, and heard the pastor say "Those whom God has joined together let no one separate." What more is there? Oh, that's right, there's the part about God's blessing. The rings may have been blessed, but now it is time to pray for God's blessings on you two.

Blessings are great. Think about your blessings for a moment. What are they? Many of us, when we contemplate our blessings, identify family, health, jobs, or vocation. You might even think to name the gift of eternal life through Jesus Christ as a blessing. We engage in blessing talk almost on a daily basis. "Bless you" or "God bless you" is the single most common response to hearing someone sneeze. At the root of those few words is the tradition to invoke God's power to grant a person good health. It comes from the thinking that blessings are the good things we receive from God.

Marriages are not always full of good things. We hope your lives together will be filled with incredible and endless joys, but the reality of our human condition tells us otherwise. You will grapple with the challenges of marriage even as you celebrate the joys. So if invoking God's power to bless your marriage doesn't guarantee a lifetime of happiness and good things, then what does it mean?

Blessings are more about relationships than they are about benefits. Throughout the scriptures, God's blessings are given on the basis and nature of relationships. God blessed the people whom he had called out of Egypt. God said to Israel through Moses:

You have seen what I did to the Egyptians, and how I bore you on eagle's wings and brought you to myself. Now, therefore, if you obey my voice and keep my covenant, you shall be my tresured possession out of all the peoples. Indeed, the whole earth is mine, but you shall be for me a priestly kingdom and a holy nation. (Exod. 19:4-6)

God delivered the people and now called them to live in a particular kind of relationship, as a priestly people and a holy nation. Through them, God would work for the benefit of the whole world. They were blessed.

Read the following marriage blessing from *Evangelical Lutheran Worship*. As you do, think about the words and the way in which they describe the relationship God has with us, and the kind of relationship we are called to have with one another.

Most gracious God, we give you thanks for your tender love in sending Jesus Christ to come among us, to be born of a human mother, and to endure the cross for our sake, that we may have abundance of life.

By the power of your Holy Spirit pour out the abundance of your blessing on _name_ and _name_. Defend them from every enemy. Lead them into all peace. Let your love be a seal upon their hearts, a mantle about their shoulders, and a crown upon their foreheads.

Bless them so that their lives together may bear witness to your love. Bless them in their work and in their companionship; in their sleeping and in their waking; in their joys and in their sorrows; in their life and in their death.

Finally, in your mercy, bring them to that table where your saints feast forever in your heavenly home, through Jesus Christ our Lord, who lives and reigns with you and the Holy Spirit, one God, now and forever.
Amen.

As with God's people Israel, God yearns to have a special relationship with you also. God created you in love. God's love was made visible in Christ. In marriage God participates in your love for one another through the Holy Spirit. In short, God wants to be a part of your new life together. You are blessed.

God's presence and real desire to participate in your life together is exciting! How could it not be? Now you are free to respond to God's gracious love by being a living reflection of God's love for humanity.

Questions for conversation

1. How will your relationship with your spouse be different because of your blessing from God?

2. How are you a blessing to one another?

3. How are you a blessing to the world?

Chapter 11

Prayers for the People: Prayers of Intercession

This day is your day. It is not unusual for the official wedding planning to have taken many months. The unofficial planning can last for years. You consider every detail. You take care of every eventuality, every possible problem. It is your day, and everyone around caters to you, your plans, and your desires.

Although this assessment may be an exaggeration, you will find few, if any, days in life in which you have so much control. Name another day when you can get your friends to buy or rent matching clothes and wear them all day!

In many ways the day is all about you, but during the marriage service something happens. Time after time the attention and focus of the worship service shifts away from you the couple and toward someone or something else. Consider this invitation into the prayers of intercession: "Seeing how greatly God has loved us, let us pray for the whole world." Once again we are turned to God and the world.

We are reminded once more of the natural flow of all things. Nothing begins with us, welling up from some secret source deep within our souls. Instead, all good things begin with God. The prayers of intercession are no different.

When we gather as the people of God to worship and pray, our attention from the very first petition is generally drawn away from ourselves. Even on the day of your wedding the notes in the marriage service remind us to pray "for the world and its needs." It is a time to celebrate, but it is also time to remember the gracious compassion of the one in whose name we gather. It is time to remember the great love of Jesus for all people. The love reflected in your marriage, certainly, and also the love with which we respond to the whole world. So we lift up the needs of this hurting world.

The prayers of intercession are rightly led by a layperson. This assisting minister visibly reminds the assembly that the prayers of all people, ordained or not, come before God with equal standing. God hears us all.

The prayers of intercession provide an opportunity for you to honor a person of faith with a significant role in your marriage service. Just as you could choose someone dear to you to be a reader, crucifer, communion assistant, or acolyte, you could choose someone to be an assisting minister. You aren't limited to selecting friends and family to serve only as groomsmen and bridesmaids. Your friends and family can be involved in worship leadership at your wedding in many ways.

Consider, too, the reality that you do not have to pray the intercessions as presented in *Evangelical Lutheran Worship*. You could, working with your pastor, write your own. What are the worries and concerns you have for creation, the world, the nations, the church, your congregation, your family and friends? In writing your own intercessions you could express to God, on a more intimate and personal level, the joys and concerns you have for God's whole creation.

Even though it is your day, the church at worship always looks beyond the physical walls of the building where it gathers to remember the needs of the last, the least, the lonely, and the lost. The prayers of intercession serve as another reminder that this day is not just about you and your wedding. It is the church at worship, and you are guests of honor at Jesus' celebration.

Questions for conversation

1. Who might you choose to participate in your wedding as a worship leader? How might they serve?

2. If you were to write the prayers of intercession for your wedding, what concerns would be important to include?

Chapter 12

A Joyful Exchange: Peace

Have you ever been hurt by someone so badly you wanted to hurt them back? If you are a human being and you are honest with yourself then you must answer "yes." We are all sinful, and we have all wanted to get revenge. If we really want to be honest with each other, then we will admit that on occasion we have given in to our desire to seek revenge.

Of course, when we have been wronged by someone we do not know well, the desire to get even is usually fleeting. For example, when someone drives aggressively in traffic and cuts you off or makes a hand gesture at you, you may be hurt and want to get back at them. But most often, our anger passes relatively quickly and we are able to carry on with our lives, eventually forgetting the incident entirely.

When you are hurt by someone who is close to you, though—a friend, sibling, parent, or fiancé—the pain caused by their behavior can last for a long, long time. You have made yourself vulnerable to them. They know you and things about you perhaps no one else does. You trust them deeply. When they hurt you, the trust is broken. That is what makes the pain so lasting.

As a married couple, you will be vulnerable to one another in ways that are not duplicated in any other relationship. You will share with your spouse your inmost fears, weaknesses, desires, hopes, and dreams for your life together. Because you will continue to know one another more deeply and intimately in your marriage, you will know those things that can hurt your spouse most profoundly.

As part of worship at your wedding, you and the assembly will have the opportunity to share the peace of Christ with one another. The words are simple:

The peace of Christ be with you always.
And also with you.

Behind these words is a call to reject any desire to seek revenge and instead pursue reconciliation. When you share the peace with one another you are acting out the reconciliation of Christ with the whole world. Extending and receiving the peace is not simply about finding and reconciling with someone you have wronged or someone who has wronged you. Sharing the peace at your wedding will help set the tone for your marriage. Consider this note on the exchange of peace in the *Evangelical Lutheran Worship* marriage rite: "After the presiding minister greets the assembly, the couple may greet each other with the kiss of peace, and the assembly may greet one another in peace."

It is becoming increasingly common for a newly married couple to exchange a kiss as their exchange of peace. It is not the traditional "You-may-kiss-the-bride" kiss, as though now it is acceptable for you to share a basic level of intimacy as a married couple. It is, in the tradition of the early church, a kiss of peace with one another. Of course you won't kiss everyone in the congregation, but this simple gesture speaks volumes about your marriage.

Whether you shake hands, hug, or kiss, the gift of peace exchanged will keep you mindful of the forgiveness and reconciliation we have in Christ and the forgiveness we are called to share with one another.

Questions for conversation

1. How are you most vulnerable to one another?

2. How will you share the peace of Christ in your marriage?

3. How will you share the peace of Christ with the world in your daily living?

Chapter 13

A Festive Feast: Holy Communion

Have you thought about the menu for your reception yet? For many couples, selecting the menu for the wedding reception is some of the most fun they have while planning their wedding. They may sit at a table in the hotel banquet hall where the reception is to be held while waiters bring out sample after sample of entrées, salads, and desserts. Will they have the chicken or beef? Will they serve seafood?

The meal at the reception is a big deal for many couples because they want to be good hosts for friends and family. They want their guests to fully enjoy themselves and be satisfied. Providing the best food and drink they can afford is one way for the couple to show their guests how important they are to them.

Of course, in the days, months, and years following your wedding, it won't be the food that your friends and family remember. What your friends and family will remember will be the fun and fellowship had over the meal during the course of the reception. The meal will bring you all together after the wedding service. It will provide an opportunity to strengthen bonds of friendship and love not only between you and your guests but among the guests themselves.

At your marriage service, you will have an opportunity to serve a much simpler meal. The menu for this meal is different but the host will be delighted to give you his very best. Read the words of institution from the holy communion liturgy:

In the night in which he was betrayed, our Lord Jesus took bread, and gave thanks; broke it, and gave it to his disciples, saying: Take and eat; this is my body, given for you. Do this for the remembrance of me.

Again, after supper, he took the cup, gave thanks, and gave it for all to drink, saying: This cup is the new covenant in my blood, shed for you and for all people for the forgiveness of sin. Do this for the remembrance of me.

Jesus is present at all tables, all altars where the sacrament of holy communion is celebrated. Indeed, he makes all meals themselves holy events.

Have you thought about whether to celebrate holy communion at your wedding and what doing so means for your marriage? Because the gift of holy communion is central to who and whose we are as Christians, and because forgiveness is a significant part of the gift from God, and because marriage requires mutual mercy and forgiveness to endure, it is indeed well and good to celebrate holy communion as part of the marriage service.

Eating the meal together with the whole assembly is a visible sign of unity and strength. In the days and weeks and years to come you will need all the strength and support you can get. It is this meal that will sustain you, as a couple and in your individual lives of faith, week in and week out throughout your lives.

Questions for conversation

1. What are some of your favorite memories that involve food?

2. What are some of the festive meals from your family history?

3. What is your response to the idea of celebrating holy communion at your wedding?

4. In what ways would celebrating holy communion change your marriage service?

Chapter 14

A Timely Thank You: Prayer after Communion

Have you registered for gifts yet? If you are like many couples preparing for marriage, you will create a wedding registry (or two) for the benefit of your guests. Of course, the registry is as much for your benefit as it is theirs. After all, as convenient as it is to cook with and clean up a George Foreman® Lean Mean Grilling Machine, you don't want more than one. The wedding registry is one way of helping your guests know just what you need as you begin your life together.

In response to your guests' generosity, it behooves you to send proper thank you notes. Aside from simply being the polite and courteous thing to do, thank you notes acknowledge the gracious generosity of your friends, family, and acquaintances who have responded to the needs you identified. Giving you what you need is one of the ways in which they show their support and express their love for you both.

As you can read below, the prayer after communion in your wedding service, if you choose to celebrate holy communion, is a thank you note of sorts to God.

> Loving God, we thank you that you have fed us in this holy meal, united us with Christ, and given us a foretaste of the heavenly banquet. So strengthen us in your service that our daily lives may show our thanks, through Jesus Christ our Lord. (*Evangelical Lutheran Worship* Leaders Edition, p. 684)

In Matthew's gospel Jesus reminds the disciples, "Your Father knows what you need before you ask him" (Matt. 6:8b). We don't have to ask God for a thing. A divine wedding registry isn't necessary. God knows what is needed and gives it to us. We need to be drawn closer to God the Father through Christ the Son. We need to experience God's forgiveness. We need a glimpse of the future hope we all share in Christ Jesus when all of creation will be fully restored in God. The gift of holy communion does these things and more. It is only appropriate that we extend our thanks to God in this prayer.

This prayer, however, isn't the only thank you that you will offer to God. Unlike the china and crystal you may receive, unpack, and tuck away in a drawer, chest, or cabinet and use mostly on special occasions, the gifts of God in this holy meal are to be used constantly. The prayer says as much. Your lives together serve as an ongoing thank you note to God. As you have been forgiven, you are called to forgive. As you have been blessed with the presence of Christ, you are to be the body of Christ to others. Lives of humble service and loving obedience to the will of God, both in how you love and serve one another, as well as how you love and serve God's people in the world are the greatest expressions of thanks we can offer our Lord.

Questions for conversation

1. What are some gifts God has given you that you knew you needed?

2. What are some gifts God has given you that you didn't know you needed?

3. What are ways in which you give thanks to God in your daily living now?

4. What are three ways in which you, as a married couple, will give thanks to God through your lives together?

Back to the Beginning: Blessing

Consider for a moment the shape of a ring. It is a circle with no beginning and no end. One point flows to another in a constant motion, totally connected, united and one. Your wedding ring will be such a circle, as each point in your life constantly draws you back to your marriage, each event in your life somehow connected to who you are as an individual and as a husband or wife. All of your life will be connected to this new, wonderful, and glorious reality.

Your wedding service will have the same sense of connectedness. The service begins with these words: "The grace of our Lord Jesus Christ, the love of God, and the communion of the Holy Spirit be with you all." Then the service ends where it began: with a prayer for the blessing of the triune God, Father, Son, and Holy Spirit to be upon you for all the days of your life. In fact, the entire worship service revolves around this central prayer. It serves as a constant reminder, woven throughout the fabric of worship, that we and all creation are wholly and completely dependent upon God for everything. This final blessing on you and the whole assembly does not pray for health, wealth, happiness, many children, large homes, or luxury cars. It asks for the difficult blessings of God.

> God Almighty send you light and truth
> to keep you all the days of your life.
> The hand of God protect you;
> the holy angels accompany you;
> and the blessing of almighty God,
> the Father, the + Son, and the Holy Spirit,
> be with you now and forever.

The light and truth of God is a gracious gift, but a difficult one to receive. As you live together and begin to know one another in a deeper and more intimate way, things will change between you. Each of you will discover parts of you that you might not be proud of. There are other things we have all done in our past we wish would stay hidden. Sometimes it is an embarrassing story from childhood, retold at every family gathering. Other memories are far darker, thoughts and regrets that haunt us. Consider your life, your past and present, and consider holding that up to the light and truth of God.

Even as you reflect on your life, know and believe in these words. In the cross of Christ those sins, those acts committed in the dark, those deeds lying in secret, have all been forgiven. That is the grace of God. That too is the blessing of God. You have been welcomed into the arms of God's mercy.

The blessing at the end of the marriage service also prays for protection and the presence of God's holy angels in your life. It is our prayer as well. May your life together, your days together, be marked by God's presence. May the love of Jesus be reflected through the love you share as husband and wife.

All these things we ask from the fullness of the holy Trinity. We trust in the completeness of God for the completion of our lives. May you live and love together, and may your love find strength, support, and encouragement through the love of God, the Father, the Son, and the Holy Spirit. Amen.

Questions for conversation

1. How might holding up the hidden parts of your life to the light and truth of God be a frightening prospect for you?

2. Where do you need the presence and protection of God's holy angels?

Chapter 16

Sent to Serve: Dismissal

The end is finally here. Or maybe it would be better to say the beginning has finally arrived. The worship service is now over, but in a sense it never ends. In congregations that end worship with a procession of the cross and worship leaders from the front of the church to the back, words of dismissal are spoken after the assembly has turned to follow the movement of the cross. Facing the doors to the street, the assembly is sent into the world.

Worship is a rehearsal for living in a world that lives differently than the church. Consider your day thus far. You have been greeted in the name of the triune God. You have heard the good news. You have been prayed for. In spite of everything you hear, throughout the service the focus has been less on you as a couple and more on God Almighty, creator of all that is. In worship we have practiced living out the love of God, holy, pure, and righteous, knowing full well our love is at best a pale reflection of God's love.

"Go in peace. Serve the Lord." These words ring in your ears as you leave the church. Not, "Go in peace. Love each other." Not, "Go in peace. Have a wonderful life together." Instead, on your wedding day you are sent to serve God. It only makes sense. Your life together as husband and wife, living, loving, learning, and growing together, is one of the many ways you serve God. Certainly volunteering in church, teaching Sunday school, or singing in the choir is service to God. Obviously, helping to build a Habitat for Humanity house serves God. No less significantly, and quite possibly more significantly, your marriage and the love and commitment you share, serves God.

At its best, your marriage, through the inevitable ups and downs, joys and sorrows, sickness and the health, good days and bad, can be for others and for you a sign of God's holy presence in this broken world. In a world in need of hope and promise, your marriage can be a light in the darkness. You serve God by loving your spouse. Did you ever think serving God could be so fun, so filled with joy, passion, and even romance?

So leave the church, go out into the world, and serve God in all aspects of your life together. Serve your God through acts of love and affection. Serve your God by being gracious, forgiving, and thoughtful. Serve your God with all of your being, with every breath and moment of your life. Your marriage, your life, and this world will be all the better for it. Thanks be to God.

Questions for conversation

1. What are some of the ways you serve God in your life?

2. How might you serve God together?

3. Whose marriages do you see reflecting God's love? How?

Part Two

Devotions for the First Twelve Months of Marriage

You made it through the big day. It is our prayer that your day was wonderful—everything you hoped it would be and more. Now that the party is over, the real fun begins. The true joy is not the parties, but the living together day in and day out and continuing to grow together in love, by the grace of God.

The following twelve chapters are intended to be read one each month for the first year of your marriage. Set aside time each month to talk with one another, practice being open and honest with your joys and struggles, and embrace the couple you are becoming.

You are in a time of great transition and change in your life. By worshiping together faithfully, gathering with the people of God regularly, praying together, and learning to love each other and Jesus, you will be blessed.

Reading these devotions together does not guarantee a perfect marriage, whatever "perfect" might mean. But reading these devotions together will strengthen your relationship with each other and with God. May your life together be blessed through these humble offerings.

Chapter 17

After the Honeymoon: Dismissal

Jesus said to [the disciples], "Peace be with you. As the Father has sent me, so I send you." (John 20:21)

Have you taken a honeymoon yet? If so, how was it? Some couples elect, by choice or necessity, to wait to take a honeymoon. In some instances honeymoons are never taken at all. Sadly, the hustle and bustle of life doesn't slow down now that you are married. In addition to life's daily grind, in your first month of marriage you are learning how to live under one roof: new routines, new patterns of living, new quirks and idiosyncrasies to discover about your new spouse. Few times in life offer so many opportunities for new discoveries. Does your spouse squeeze the toothpaste tube from the middle or the bottom? Which side of the bed will you be sleeping on? Choose wisely; it will probably be the side you sleep on for the rest of your life. Believe it or not, rather innocuous things like these have been points of contention for more than a few couples.

Have you experienced some of these little struggles in your marriage yet? Recall for a moment how your wedding service ended. Consider again the final words with which the assembly was sent forth, and your response:

Go in peace. Serve the Lord.
Thanks be to God.

These final words of the marriage service are not simply offered as kind words for well-being and happiness in your marriage. The dismissal is an instruction on how to live faithfully with one another and with God. In faithful living, God is served.

You were sent with God's peace. The Hebrew word for peace is shalom. Shalom is God's peace. This peace is more than just getting along. Shalom means actively pursuing harmony within relationships. Shalom means forgiving and allowing ourselves to be forgiven. Shalom means loving and allowing ourselves to be loved. Shalom is happening when God is restoring what was broken and strengthening what is joined together.

Shalom is not something that just happens on its own, but intentionally. St. Paul writes in Romans 14:19, "Let us then pursue what makes for peace and mutual upbuilding." Your honeymoon was (or will be) a gift for this reason. You set a precedent when you made time for one another. Continue making time for one another. You might wish your honeymoon could be a week off from your job each month. As wonderful as that may sound your boss might not approve! You can, however, have a daily honeymoon—that is, taking time each day to follow St. Paul's instruction to pursue those things that make for peace and mutual upbuilding. Actively listen to one another, pray for and with one another, be romantic, and especially worship together with God's people.

Consider, too, the peace you share with one another is not for you to hoard. With the strength of your new marriage you are invited, urged, called, and sent by God out into the world to care for others with the love and peace of Jesus. This service will take various forms. For some people it is reflected through service in their congregation. For others it is lived out by volunteering for community organizations that feed the hungry or shelter the homeless. It may mean encouraging others when their marriages are fragile or failing, reminding friends of their marriage vows when they might be tempted to stray, and helping to strengthen all marriages through your words and actions. In doing these things, you will find that the honeymoon isn't over and your service to the Lord never ends. Thanks be to God!

Questions for conversation

1. How do you make time for one another?

2. How does your time together create peace in your marriage?

Prayer

God of peace, you love your whole creation and you desire us to live so that the joy of your gospel may be visible to all. Fill us with your peace. Comfort us with your Holy Spirit. Strengthen us with your love. Continue to bless our marriage with your presence that we may know your peace and carry your love into the world. In Jesus' name we pray. Amen.

Chapter 18

Month Two: Blessing

Nothing is covered up that will not be uncovered, and nothing secret that will not become known. Therefore whatever you have said in the dark will be heard in the light. (Luke 12:2-3)

Toward the end of your marriage service, these or similar words of blessing were prayed over you and the assembly:

God Almighty send you light and truth
to keep you all the days of your life.
The hand of God protect you;
the holy angels accompany you;
and the blessing of almighty God,
the Father, the + Son, and the Holy Spirit,
be with you now and forever.

Why, of all things, ask God for light? Then again, have you ever thought about the power of light? Light has the remarkable ability to be both harmful and protective. Too much light, focused too intensely, can blind your eyes or burn your skin. Just the right amount of light can provide a sense of security. The flickering light from candles at a dinner can create a wonderfully peaceful and romantic mood. The flashing of lightning in the dark of night can throw shadows that terrify a child.

This blessing asks for your wedded life to be illuminated by the light of God. The light of God in your marriage can be terrifying but it can also be protective. God's light can be terrifying because light exposes secrets. Light exposes the things we want to remain covered. It reveals the things we want to keep hidden. You will be tempted, as all human beings are, to keep things from your spouse. They may be things you have done or not done, said or not said. You know the secrets you are tempted to keep.

Remember, nothing grows in darkness. Secrets will kill relationships, and the more invested in the relationship and the bigger the secret, the more deadly it can become. Still, we fear the light of truth, we fear revealing ourselves completely, certain if we do we will be rejected. So we invite the darkness into our lives.

On your wedding day the assembly added its "Amen!" to the prayer for God's light to shine in your marriage. The light of God shines into the deepest chasms and the tiniest cracks of your marriage. God takes an interest in every part of your relationship. Even in the smallest places and in the tiniest ways in which we may want to welcome darkness, we pray such darkness would be dispelled by the light of Jesus.

The light of God is protective in your marriage. God's light protects you from the darkness that could be invited in. When the darkness isn't welcome, secrets aren't kept, and those things that could create anxiety in your marriage are kept at bay.

One of the simplest and most effective means of welcoming God's light into your marriage is through open, honest, loving, compassionate, and perhaps sometimes frank conversation. This type of communication is necessary. Words are at the heart of how the light of God is revealed in the world. Consider what the world would be like if no one ever spoke the good news of the gospel. Darkness would rule the day. In your marriage, open, honest, and loving speech welcomes the light of God as it welcomes the light of the gospel.

It can be difficult to be open and honest with your spouse, particularly when emotions are running high. You may be angry, hurt, resentful, fearful of a reaction, or just uncertain about how to speak. In those times, the rays of God's light yearn to burst forth. The Holy Spirit will guide you to resist the temptation to clam up and keep feelings, thoughts, and concerns bottled up inside. Trust in the abiding promise of God to sustain and support you that God's light may shine in your marriage throughout your lives.

Questions for conversation

1. How do you speak openly and honestly with one another?

2. What can you do to improve your communication so that the light of God may be more welcome in your marriage?

Prayer

God of light and truth, come to us. In your compassion bless us and fill our marriage with your light. Dispel the darkness that creeps into our lives. Bless us with words of support, hope, and love, through Jesus Christ our Lord. Amen.

Chapter 19

Month Three: Peace

Peace I leave with you; my peace I give to you. I do not give to you as the world gives. Do not let your hearts be troubled, and do not let them be afraid. (John 14:27)

When you are in conversation with another person and you make reference to "my wife" or "my husband," do you mentally pause and think about the significance of those two simple words? At first it might feel odd, awkward, or even strange to speak of your spouse. It is new vocabulary for you. As these weeks turn into months and months to years, talking about "my wife" or "my husband" will come to feel more natural, more comfortable. It is not simply a function of time, however; it also grows out of the depth of your relationship. As a newly married couple your relationship is in transition. For three brief months you have been different from how you were before.

Think back to the days when you first started dating. What did it feel like when you introduced the one who is now your spouse as your boyfriend or your girlfriend? Later, once you were engaged, recall the feeling of introducing your fiancé. Did it feel a little exciting when you said that? Did it sound strange coming out of your mouth? Over time, as your relationship developed and deepened, saying "my fiancé" didn't sound strange any longer. It sounded natural, and you felt a sense of comfort in knowing this person was your partner.

Now you don't introduce your companion as your boyfriend or girlfriend or fiancé. Those terms are no longer adequate. You are learning to find a particular comfort in your relationship again.

At your wedding service, the pastor, speaking in Christ's name, exchanged a greeting of peace with the gathered assembly.

The peace of Christ be with you always.

And also with you.

This same exchange of peace happens each time your congregation celebrates holy communion. In this simple exchange of peace the pastor expresses Christ's desire to be a part of the deepening and strengthening of your relationship. Not only was that exchange for you two but it was for the relationships of everyone gathered at your wedding. Each time you share the peace in worship you invite Christ to be a part of your relationship, strengthening, deepening, and sustaining it.

As you grow together in marriage, Christ will be an ever-present giver of his peace. Through this peace, it is our prayer that you find comfort in one another. It is our prayer that as each day passes your relationship will continue to feel more natural.

In the same way, we pray that as you grow together in marriage you will sense how Christ is drawing himself closer to you—through word, sacrament, worship, and the companionship of friends and family. Here the peace of Christ will be with you always.

Questions for conversation

1. What are some ways in which you have found greater comfort in one another as your relationship has deepened in marriage?

2. How has Christ supported and sustained your marriage so far?

Prayer

Lord God, giver of good things and sustainer of all that you have made, bless us now with the gift of your peace. Strengthen us as we grow together in marriage. May we, through your Son, Jesus Christ our Lord, find in you comfort in our days together. Amen.

Chapter 20

Month Four: Prayers of Intercession

Then Jesus called the twelve together and gave them power and authority over all demons and to cure diseases, and he sent them out to proclaim the kingdom of God and to heal. (Luke 9:1-2)

What was the last gift or loving gesture that you shared with your spouse? How are you at saying "I love you" to one another? Many discussions of marriage focus almost completely on the couple, their relationship, their difficulties, and their mutual joys. Certainly it is important for the two of you to care for one another, love one another, and attend to your marriage. Still, in all this talk of you, you face the danger of allowing no room for anyone else.

Throughout your engagement and for the first few months of marriage your relationship was likely, well, mostly about you. First it was all about planning the wedding and preparing for your special day. You created a guest list, chose flowers, registered for gifts, and so on. Now, as a married couple, you continue the decision-making process. This process has and will continue to have a profound impact on your lives together. These decisions are as simple as who will take out the trash and as potentially emotional as how and with whom to celebrate holidays.

Your focus has been on you and your life together. But hopefully it has included more than a little consideration of how Christ is a part of your marriage. Hopefully you have asked yourselves how Jesus strengthens and supports you through word, sacrament, and the gathered assembly of believers in worship. Hopefully you are ready and open to consider how you as a couple relate to the world around you.

Do you remember the prayers for the world and its needs at your wedding? In the *Evangelical Lutheran Worship* marriage rite, each petition in the prayers of intercession concludes:

Gracious and faithful God,
hear our prayer.

You may not have given these prayers much thought since then. However, their placement in the wedding service was significant and intentional. Immediately following the blessing of your marriage, the assembly was invited into these prayers. As soon as the big event happened the spotlight shifted from you and focused on the whole world. You had not even been married for five minutes and the assembly had its focus redirected. You have only been married four months and we are refocusing your attention.

Being loving and compassionate toward one another is wonderful and should be commended. Allowing Christ to guide you to serve one another in a faithful way is a beautiful thing. But as Christ's disciples we are called to serve lovingly and compassionately in the world around us, too. The prayers of intercession were the beginning of that process. In them you and all those gathered prayed that you might be the body of Christ in the world. You prayed that you might be instruments of God's peace. You prayed for those who are lonely, sick, dying, poor, hungry, homeless, unemployed, victims of violence, hatred, and intolerance.

You took the first steps in these prayers to serve God faithfully by serving others in God's name. Now it is time you consider how you might live those prayers out. How can you be the body of Christ in the world? How can you be instruments of God's peace? How can you serve those who need the blessed good news of the gospel?

You could serve God together in many ways in the world and community around you. However, let us suggest that you find an outreach ministry in your congregation and together actively participate in it. Does your congregation have a food pantry? Bag some groceries! Do folks sing Christmas carols at local nursing homes? Sing your heart out! Seek out ways to live out your baptismal calling together and be active in the outreach ministry of your church. And if you are completely stumped, ask your pastor.

He or she will welcome the conversation. You are called to live out your baptismal calling within the life of the congregation as well, which means responding faithfully to the call to worship, giving generously of your financial resources, sharing your faith through teaching, worship leadership, and other forms of serving in your home congregation.

May your lives be living examples of the prayers you speak.

Questions for conversation

1. What are some of your congregation's outreach ministries in which you can get involved?

2. When will you see your pastor again so that you may offer yourselves to the service of the church?

3. How will you support your church's ministries financially?

Prayer

Most holy God, you send us forth to serve your whole creation in humble obedience. Strengthen us in our marriage, guide us in godly living, and create in us the will to proclaim your kingdom through our words and actions, through Jesus Christ our Lord, who lives and reigns with you and the Holy Spirit, one God, now and forever. Amen.

Chapter 21

Month Five: Marriage Blessing

> Then [Jesus] looked up at his disciples and said: "Blessed are you who are poor, for yours is the kingdom of God. Blessed are you who are hungry now, for you will be filled. Blessed are you who weep now, for you will laugh.
>
> Blessed are you when people hate you, and when they exclude you, revile you, and defame you on account of the Son of Man. Rejoice in that day and leap for joy, for surely your reward is great in heaven; for that is what their ancestors did to the prophets." (Luke 6:20-23)

What has been the biggest surprise in your marriage so far? More specifically, what has surprised you most about your spouse? Is there something your spouse has done for you that was surprisingly gracious? Did you just discover he or she can make the most wonderfully perfect omelets? Or has there been a less wonderful surprise? Does your husband (or wife) snore like a bear? Have you been banished to the couch because your snoring seems likely to create vibrations strong enough to shift the foundation of the building?

At your wedding, the pastor prayed in the marriage blessing for God to send the Holy Spirit to bless you. This blessing wasn't just for the good stuff. It wasn't a prayer that God, through the Holy Spirit, would bless the good in your relationship and curse the bad. Hear the words of the blessing once more:

> Most gracious God, we give you thanks for your tender love in sending Jesus Christ to come among us, to be born of a human mother, and to endure the cross for our sake, that we may have abundance of life.
>
> By the power of your Holy Spirit pour out the abundance of your blessing on *name* and *name*. Defend them from every

enemy. Lead them into all peace. Let your love be a seal upon their hearts, a mantle about their shoulders, and a crown upon their foreheads.

Bless them so that their lives together may bear witness to your love. Bless them in their work and in their companionship; in their sleeping and in their waking; in their joys and in their sorrows; in their life and in their death.

Finally, in your mercy, bring them to that table where your saints feast forever in your heavenly home, through Jesus Christ our Lord, who lives and reigns with you and the Holy Spirit, one God, now and forever.

This blessing begins with a reminder of the gift of resurrected life coming to us through the suffering, death, and resurrection of our Lord Jesus Christ. Before you think of yourselves, remember the one who has already done everything for us. The blessing continues with a prayer for protection. We all yearn for God's protection.

In the next paragraph, however, things get a little strange. The pastor asks that you be blessed in your joys and sorrows, in your life and in your death. It might be hard to imagine why we would pray to be blessed even in our sorrows and in our death.

You may recall, however, that blessings are about strengthening relationships. Sometimes our relationships are strengthened more by the struggles we experience than by the joys. The two of you are learning how to be open and honest with one another. It might mean having the courage to send your snoring spouse to the couch for a night. In the middle of the night such honesty might not be welcome, but it will benefit you both in the long run. Indeed, part of an honest and open relationship means the willingness to risk short-term pain for long-term gains.

As you sort out what it means to be married to one another and live together you will share joys, sorrows, and struggles. You just might discover that through those struggles and the sometimes difficult conversations, your relationship grows in new and beautiful ways. You might come to see some of those challenges as gifts from God.

Of course the joys are blessings as well. One of the blessed joys God gives us is the joy of community. The gathered people of God are your brothers and sisters in Christ. This blessing is easy to forget, easy to miss and—when things are difficult—easy to abandon. Yet, come what may, this community is here to support your marriage and point you to the hope of Jesus.

The end of the marriage blessing reminds us that God's greatest promise is the promise of resurrected life. It is the promise that puts all the rest of life in context. The future is in God's hands. Come what may, you belong to God.

As you continue to live and grow in marriage, may you discover the wonder and joy of the blessings of God and be strengthened by them in your life together.

Questions for conversation

1. What difficulties or challenges have you been surprised to discover actually strengthened your relationship?

2. How have you sensed the presence of the Holy Spirit blessing your marriage?

Prayer

Heavenly Father, our lives are filled with joys and sorrows. From the peaks of our highest highs to the depths of our lowest lows, you are with us. Help us to see in all things the gift of your blessing. May we, through all of life's experiences, be strengthened in our marriage by your Holy Spirit. For we live and work and have our being in you. In Jesus' name we pray. Amen.

Chapter 22

Month Six: Acclamation

So they are no longer two, but one flesh. Therefore what God has joined together, let no one separate. (Matt. 19:6)

Name and *name*, by their promises before God
and in the presence of this assembly,
have joined themselves to one another as husband and wife.
Those whom God has joined together let no one separate.
Amen. Thanks be to God.

What a joyous moment in your lives! Those words publicly acclaimed you as a married couple. Nothing could stand in your way! In fact, the pastor said as much: "Those whom God has joined together let no one separate." What a powerful statement. That simple statement will bring more joy to your marriage than the public announcement of your marriage.

"Those whom God has joined together let no one separate" speaks of God's continued presence in your lives as a couple. You bound yourselves to one another in marriage but God made it permanent. You may think, "Not all marriages are permanent." With the sad reality of divorce, you are certainly correct. But God's commitment to sustain, uplift, strengthen, and guide your married lives is permanent. You have bound yourselves to one another but you got bound up with God in the bargain. In this way getting married is similar to being baptized. In holy baptism, you are bound to God in a permanent way. It can never be undone.

Similarly, the promises you have made can never be undone. Every marriage experiences troublesome periods. Maybe trouble lasts a few minutes or maybe it is a few months. You may actually experience such difficulty in your marriage that you wish you had never made those promises at all. You may even act like you had not made them. Because human beings are in bondage to sin, they will never be able to keep their promises fully. Only God can fully keep promises. Still, on your wedding day you made promises to God and one another that cannot be taken back.

Your family and friends, the whole assembly, in fact, made promises at your wedding. They were included in the declaration of intention. With a resounding "We will," all those gathered promised "by God's grace to uphold and care for" you both in your life together. The assembly cannot take its promises back, either. Everyone involved in your wedding made promises. They may live out those promises through prayer, gifts, or conversation. Whatever they do, their promises cannot be undone nor can they be taken back. Throughout your life together the whole community of faith continues to be available to you.

So here, after six months of marriage, we return to the acclamation. We return to the first announcement of your marriage. We return to what was certainly one of the most joyous moments of your wedding day. We return here to point you forward to the days to come. We return here that you may be reminded of the joyous promises of fidelity and support made by you, by the assembly, and by God. Yes, it is true that you may face some bumpy roads ahead. But you won't travel them alone, for God Almighty, the creator of all that is, has seen fit to take an interest in you and your marriage. What an awesome gift! Even as you work together, and learn how to be a married couple, God too is working on your behalf through the gracious Holy Spirit. Indeed, if God is for you, who can be against you? Thanks be to God!

Questions for conversation

1. What are some promises you have kept in your marriage that have brought you joy?

2. How does the church support your marriage?

3. In what ways do you sense God's support in your marriage?

Prayer

Most High God, you support and sustain all of your creation. Continue to support and sustain our marriage, that through your holy church we may know the joy of your presence, through Jesus Christ our Lord, who lives and reigns with you and the Holy Spirit, one God, now and forever. Amen.

Chapter 23

Month Seven: Giving of Rings

So then you are no longer strangers and aliens, but you are citizens with the saints and also members of the household of God, built upon the foundation of the apostles and prophets, with Christ Jesus himself as the cornerstone. In him the whole structure is joined together and grows into a holy temple in the Lord; in whom you also are built together spiritually into a dwelling place for God. (Eph. 2:19-22)

Remember what your wedding rings looked like when you first exchanged them? They were probably just about perfect, without scar or blemish. Not a scratch or nick on the surface, and bright and shiny as they could be. Just like your marriage.

How do they look today? How have they held up to the abuse that comes with daily wearing? They probably show a few scratches on the surface. Your ring might not be quite as bright and shiny as it was the day of your wedding. But there it is nonetheless, on your finger, with you wherever you go.

Today your marriage is different from what it was seven months ago. Your life together has been through some changes. You know some of the ups and downs, the joys and challenges of living together. You have had to sort out washing the clothes and preparing dinner. You have had to negotiate bill paying and grocery shopping. You might have had to learn how to share the TV remote control!

Through all of these daily interactions your relationship has changed. As St. Paul writes in Ephesians 2, you are no longer strangers or aliens but now you are joined together in Christ. Slowly but surely your interactions today are shaping your way of being together and relating for years to come.

As you have had these months to begin to know one another more intimately, more deeply, you may have discovered things about each other you cherish even more. You may have discovered some of those special little joys you only learn from living together. You may have also discovered a few habits that drive you mad.

In a way, all these discoveries are like your wedding rings. The nicks and scratches might remind you of the difficult times together, of angry nights or mornings of frustration. Those scratches remain only on the surface. Below it all is the solid metal of your love, made solid not by human doing but by the grace and mercy of God.

You might have found your ring has grown more comfortable on your finger. That little ring has become more a part of you. In the same way your marriage has become basic to who you are. Who are you? You are a child of God, a dwelling place for God, a husband or wife, and many other things as well.

Now for the big question: Do you know what it feels like to take your ring off even for a few moments? By now it may feel strange and awkward. Even though you can take your ring off and put it back on, you now know your marriage is with you wherever you go, whether you wear a ring or not.

By the seventh month of your marriage, life has changed dramatically. There is this other person to relate to and discuss life with. There is this other person to be considered as decisions and plans are made. There is this other person to support you and care for you in good times and bad. May the ring you wear always remind you of your marriage and of the presence of Jesus who is with you even to the end of time.

Questions for conversation

1. How have you dealt with the joys and challenges of living together as husband and wife?

2. What are some of the wonderful and less-than-wonderful aspects of each other you have discovered?

Prayer

Holy and gracious God, you give us the gift of marriage, and promise to be with us always. Strengthen and support us in our love for one another and our commitment to our marriage. May the rings we wear remind us always of the precious gift of marriage and of one another. These things we pray through your Son, our Lord and Savior, Jesus Christ. Amen.

Chapter 24

Month Eight: Vows

Adam and Eve were in the Garden of Eden when they each ate the forbidden fruit from the tree in the center of the garden. When they ate the fruit, "Then the eyes of both were opened, and they knew that they were naked." (Gen. 3:7)

The first months of a marriage are eye-opening. Slowly but surely the insanity and passion and intensity that led up to your wedding day fades. You go to sleep and wake up eight months later and there stands your spouse, naked, with eyes wide open. For most people this sort of exposure, physical or emotional, is frightening. It calls for deep trust in the other. In marriage this trust is grounded in the commitment of love and fidelity you made to one another on the day you were married. Do you remember the vows you made to one another on that day? Do you remember everything you promised one another in the presence of God and your friends and family?

Whether you remember the exact wording or not, your promises most likely reflected at least the themes of these vows. Read through them, silently or aloud to one another, again.

In the presence of God and this community,
I, _name_, take you, _name_, to be my _wife/husband_;
to have and to hold from this day forward,
in joy and in sorrow, in plenty and in want, in sickness and in health,
to love and to cherish, as long as we both shall live.
This is my solemn vow.

By now you have seen joy and sorrow, plenty and want, sickness and health to some degree. As your lives together continue you will know all of these things more deeply, more intimately. With the experiences of the past eight months to draw from, consider how your understanding of marriage and your relationship with one another has changed.

These vows are challenging and all-encompassing. If you are honest you have already failed to keep these promises completely. When those moments happen in your marriage, it is as though your eyes are opened and you see each other in all your nakedness.

The humbling confession we all must make is that alone we cannot completely keep these vows. Too many temptations lurk in this world. Too many selfish motivations, too much selfish ambition make sharing a life completely just too hard.

At the same time, your life holds much to celebrate. You made it this far together. You continue to think and pray about your relationship. You are growing in love and affection; you are growing in trust and confidence in one another. You are finding the courage to stand before one another naked and unafraid.

You will not find strength, encouragement, and support for your marriage only by searching deep within yourself. If you only look in that place, you will be found wanting. Instead, hear the call to turn toward the one who is completely and fully faithful, even to the point of death. Turn to Jesus, pray for strength to be faithful, pray for the courage to trust, pray for the grace to forgive.

Each morning as you wake to a new day of married life, recall the promises you made to one another. Consider each day how you might live up to the awesome promises you made for the good of your life together. Each day consider all the ways your spouse has already been faithful and celebrate with joy the life you are building together. God is at work in your life yesterday, today, and tomorrow, molding and shaping you, guiding and leading you into a life of faithfulness to your marriage and to Jesus. Thanks be to God.

Questions for conversation

1. What new meaning do your marriage vows hold for each of you now?

2. How is your daily life shaped by your marriage vows?

Prayer

God of grace and glory, you have given us the gift of one another. Deepen our love for you and for each other, and give us the courage to stand naked and unafraid before one another, that we may live in fidelity to our marriage vows as long as we both shall live. This we pray in the holy name of Jesus Christ, our Lord. Amen.

Chapter 25

Month Nine: Prayer of the Day

Seven times a day I praise you for your righteous ordinances. (Ps. 119:164)

Your marriage began in prayer. During the worship service prayers washed over the two of you from the prayer of the day to the marriage blessing, to the prayers of intercession to all of the blessings in between. These prayers soaked you both with the merciful love of God. Your marriage began in prayer.

Now you are in the midst of daily life. Thanks be to God you have found the time and made the commitment to your marriage to work through this book. Still, if you are like most people your lives are filled to overflowing. It is hard to get all of the little errands and responsibilities taken care of each day. Days are long and full and time for little extras runs short.

In the early church, Christians learned to frame their day in prayer. Drawing on ancient Jewish practice, Christians were called to pray seven times each day. From the wee hours before the rising of the sun until it was time for bed, many Christians would stop what they were doing seven distinct times each day in order to pray. It may seem crazy to us, but it is a practice that continues in many Christian and non-Christian communities around the world.

Do you set aside time to pray? Does prayer guide and influence your life and the decisions you make? Do not worry about feeling guilty if you answered "no" to either of those questions. It is human to get caught up in the busy-ness of life. It is human to see the morning disappear in a rush of getting dressed, getting breakfast, and getting to work. The evenings get filled as well, with commuting and dinner, household responsibilities, volunteer work, errands, and more. With all these things going on (and children and their demands have not even been mentioned), it is little surprise most people do not make time for prayer. But if your marriage began in prayer it only makes sense to sustain it through prayer as well.

Such prayer is not as difficult as you might think. The prayers from your wedding are a wonderful place to begin. Consider the prayer of the day from your wedding service. Change just one word in the prayer and it will speak to your marriage from day to day even as it spoke to you on the day of your wedding. Here is the prayer again, with the word "marriage" substituted for the word "wedding."

> Eternal God, our creator and redeemer, as you gladdened the wedding at Cana in Galilee by the presence of your Son, so bring your joy to this marriage by his presence now. Look in favor upon _name_ and _name_ and grant that they, rejoicing in all your gifts, may at length celebrate the unending marriage feast with Christ our Lord, who lives and reigns with you and the Holy Spirit, one God, now and forever.

Imagine each day begun by inviting Jesus into your marriage. Imagine each day begun with a reminder of the God's gifts to you. You could copy the prayer, tape it to your bathroom mirror, and pray these powerful words as you start your day.

Then, at midday, perhaps at the beginning of your lunch break, pause and pray for your spouse. The words don't have to be eloquent or lengthy. You need not be concerned about the "right thing" to say. Stop, think about your beloved spouse and pray for him or her. Your prayer may be as simple as "Loving God, I give you thanks for _name_ and pray that _her/his_ day be blessed by you, in Jesus' name. Amen."

At the close of the day consider returning to the prayer with which you began your day. Even if you don't go to bed at the same time, as the first person retires for the night, pray together. You may choose another form of prayer. It's up to you. But consider the discipline of framing your day in prayer together. You may find praying with each other to be a wonderful way to remember the gift of your marriage.

Questions for conversation

1. How does prayer shape your life?

2. How does prayer for your marriage affect your relationship with your spouse and with Jesus?

3. How is your spouse a gift to you from God?

Prayer

Eternal God, our creator and redeemer, as you gladdened the wedding at Cana in Galilee by the presence of your Son, so bring your joy to our marriage by his presence now. Look in favor upon us and grant that we, rejoicing in all your gifts, may at length celebrate the unending marriage feast with Christ our Lord, who lives and reigns with you and the Holy Spirit, one God, now and forever. Amen.

Chapter 26

Month Ten: Declaration of Intention

> But we appeal to you, brothers and sisters, to respect those who labor among you, and have charge of you in the Lord and admonish you; esteem them very highly in love because of their work. Be at peace among yourselves. And we urge you, beloved, to admonish the idlers, encourage the faint hearted, help the weak, be patient with all of them. See that none of you repays evil for evil, but always seek to do good to one another and to all. Rejoice always, pray without ceasing, give thanks in all circumstances; for this is the will of God in Christ Jesus for you. (1 Thess. 5:12-18)

Do you remember the promises your family and friends made to you on your wedding day? The worship service may well have been a blur, but in the midst of everything else, before the sermon and before your vows, before you were married, your friends and family publicly promised to support your marriage. Specifically, here is what they promised:

Will you, the families of _name_ and _name_, give your love and blessing to this new family?
The families respond: We will.

Will all of you, by God's grace, uphold and care for _name_ and _name_ in their life together?
The assembly responds: **We will.**

So, how have they done? Has your family given their love and blessing to your marriage? Welcoming a new member into a family is not always an easy or smooth process. The dynamics are different, more chairs are needed for Thanksgiving dinner, another person needs to be accounted for in planning. And sometimes the members of your family are not the easiest people in the world to deal with.

It is not unheard of for these new relationships to be a source of tension and stress within a marriage. Regardless of how you feel about your family, whether it is your family of origin or the family you have married into, they are yours forever. No matter what happens they will be part of your marriage. So whatever challenges they present you may as well begin the hard work of figuring out how to live together.

One of the great challenges in marriage is that most of the things that cause trouble for couples are not temporary. Most of the problems you will face are chronic. Consider financial challenges. No matter what your income it is always possible for spending to exceed it. Until you deal with your relationship to money and the stuff in your life, the issue will always be there. Even some of the very rich still manage to spend more than they earn.

Everyone present at your wedding was invited to promise to uphold and care for you in your life together. It is a powerful and significant promise, but it is one which no one is able to fully live out. Not on their own. We turn not to our human wisdom, our human insight, and our human gifts, but instead to God. Notice the promise is made not by our own power but "by God's grace."

Now you are doing more than trusting your friends and their varying degrees of helpfulness. Now you are placing your trust in the only one who can be trusted, now you are trusting God Almighty. You turn to people not as resident experts, but as messengers of God, holy angels bearing words of confidence, promise, and hope. You turn to your brothers and sisters in Christ in hopes that they will do more than validate your feelings or agree with you. You turn to fellow Christians in hopes that they will remind you of the commitments you made to one another on the day of your wedding.

You do not need to hang on to your guest registry to know who to turn to in your time of need. The assembly, as part of the body of Christ, did not speak only for themselves. In a very real and powerful way they spoke—whether five or five hundred—for the whole of the body of Christ. The whole church on earth, the church throughout the world has pledged its support of your marriage. What an awesome gift to you. You are not alone, and whatever church you worship in, wherever Christians are gathered, you will find faithful people who promise to support you in your marriage.

Questions for conversation

1. How has your spouse's family given their love and blessing to your marriage?

2. How have they been a challenge?

3. When has the body of Christ upheld and cared for you in your life together?

4. Where do you find reminders of God's grace?

Prayer

Holy and merciful God, you give us the gift of a community of faith to uphold us in our marriage. Guide us to seek out wise and faithful counsel and open our eyes to see the strength of the body of Christ throughout the world; through Christ our Lord. Amen.

Chapter 27

Month Eleven: Introduction

> As you therefore have received Christ Jesus the Lord, continue to live your lives in him, rooted and built up in him and established in the faith, just as you were taught, abounding in thanksgiving. (Col. 2:6-7)

You have probably seen an older couple wearing matching sweaters or T-shirts commemorating their last trip to Branson, Missouri. Maybe they took the biblical image of two becoming one flesh a little too seriously! At this point in your marriage you probably do not dress alike, at least not yet, but you may be finding ways you are becoming more similar.

This idea of two becoming one flesh is not about wearing matching outfits, thinking the same thoughts, or liking the same foods. It is an image of the commitment you share for your marriage. As these months turn into years, by the grace of God, you will find the bond you share is deeper than love, deeper than feelings or emotions. You have formed a family, with or without children, and now you are connected together, through Jesus.

This connection is part of what the introduction to the marriage service points to:

> Dear friends: We have come together in the presence of God to witness the marriage of _name_ and _name_, to surround them with our prayers, and to share in their joy.

> The scriptures teach us that the bond and covenant of marriage is a gift of God in which a man and a woman are joined as one, an image of the union of Christ and the church. As _name_ and _name_ make their promises to each other today, we remember that at Cana in Galilee our Lord Jesus Christ made the wedding feast a sign of God's reign of love.

Let us enter into this celebration confident that, through the Holy Spirit, Christ is present with us now also. We pray that this couple may fulfill God's purpose for the whole of their lives. (*Evangelical Lutheran Worship* Leaders Edition, p. 676)

In your journey of married life you have the privilege of knowing another human being more deeply, more intimately than ever before. Sharing your hopes and dreams, your fears and foibles day after day will do more to draw you together than a closet full of matching sweatshirts. So consider the type of life you wish to share with your spouse. Do you want someone with whom to share a house or a home?

After coming this far with this book it is clear you want more than a silent someone sharing a house. So continue in this path in your marriage. Be intentional in your life together. Make time to share your lives. Turn off the TV, play a game of cards together and laugh; listen to music and talk. Share the stories of your life with each other, and trust that in those times when you go to places of darkness and fear, of anxiety and turmoil, Jesus himself is there with you. His love is supporting your love for one another. His presence is with you calming your fears, easing your doubts, and bringing you hope.

Questions for conversation

1. How are you intentional about sharing your lives?

2. How are you becoming one flesh?

3. How do you allow for differences?

Prayer

Gracious God, you created human beings for relationships characterized by trust, openness, and grace. By the presence of your Son Jesus in our lives, give us the courage, confidence, and faith to share our lives, our hopes and fears, our joys and sorrows, completely with one another; through Christ our Lord. Amen.

Your First Anniversary: Greeting

Finally, beloved, whatever is true, whatever is honorable, whatever is just, whatever is pure, whatever is pleasing, whatever is commendable, if there is any excellence and if there is anything worthy of praise, think about these things. Keep on doing the things that you have learned and received and heard and seen in me, and the God of peace will be with you. (Phil. 4:8-9)

Once upon a time there was a man. He was a father and a husband. He was responsible for maintaining the family cars. The family minivan was in need of an oil change and other servicing, but he ignored the odometer and the idiot lights and continued to drive the car. His wife, in frustration, finally gave up reminding him, and so it came to pass that the engine seized up and died.

Soon after the death of the beloved family minivan, the reason for his negligence came to light. It seems this husband and father had been distracted by demands from his work. Not to mention he was busy keeping up with his children, driving them from place to place, from soccer game to soccer game. Add to the equation a strained marriage and keeping secret a newfound lust for a co-worker, and it is not hard to understand why he forgot to change the oil.

You might say, with some accuracy, he spent as much time and energy in caring for his car as he did for caring for his family and marriage. In the end both car and marriage died. Cars need maintenance if they are to continue to run well for years. Your marriage requires regular servicing as well. Ignore your marriage long enough and it will die. It may not end in divorce, as this marriage did, but it can become a living death.

So your journey through these devotions ends where it began, with the simple prayer that the grace of the triune God be present in your life together as husband and wife. Here are those words once more:

The grace of our Lord Jesus Christ, the love of God,
and the communion of the Holy Spirit be with you all.
And also with you.

This continues to be our prayer for you and for your marriage. Regardless of what you do, how you communicate, how you care for one another, God's grace will surround you and support you. Yet even with all this support, marriage remains a fragile gift. It is a bond between human beings after all, and we have a habit of messing up God's gifts.

So cherish your marriage. Adore your spouse. Just think, in your spouse you have someone to care for you and share your life. Look at your spouse and see someone with whom to grow and explore God's wonderful creation. The best things in life come to us through the relationships we share. The deeper those relationships, the greater the trust and confidence you have in someone, the more fully you enter into the joy of God's creation.

Your marriage is a gift. So pay attention to the gift. Do not take it for granted. Do not miss a single opportunity to tell your new spouse how much you love him or her. Consider each day as another gift of time to spend together, to learn even more of the wonders of this person who loves and trusts you enough to commit his or her life to you.

Marriage is an awesome responsibility. By the grace of our Lord Jesus Christ, may you embrace the blessings of this gift and cherish your life together. Marriage is filled with deep and abiding joys. May the love of God draw you ever deeper into the love you share. Marriage is a holy bond, creating a new family. May the communion of the Holy Spirit give you the confidence to stand naked in every way before one another and live unafraid.

Questions for conversation

1. What do you cherish most about your spouse?

2. What do you do each day to strengthen your marriage?

3. How will you celebrate the marriage God has blessed you with?

Prayer

Lord of life, your grace has brought us together as husband and wife. May we always cherish the gift we have found in you and in each other. With the dawn of each day may we discover anew the joy of married life, that in all we do we may praise and glorify you; in Jesus' name we pray. Amen.

Chapter 29

In the End: Baptism

Then he said to me, "It is done! I am the Alpha and the Omega, the beginning and the end. To the thirsty I will give water as a gift from the spring of the water of life." (Rev. 21:6)

So here you are. You have reached the end of this devotional book together. It has been a long journey. Do you remember when you started using this book? You had so many things to think about, so many decisions to make. You weren't even married yet. Now, more than a year later you are married. You have finished. But then, you haven't really finished. You have finished this book but you are still on your life's journey as baptized, married children of God.

Martin Luther said, "When you wash your face, remember your baptism." Our lives are a daily return to our baptism. Every day we wash dirt from our face, hands, and bodies. In baptism God washed us clean and forgave us for a lifetime of sin. Baptism is where this book began and that is where we now end.

God, who is rich in mercy and love, gives us a new birth into a living hope through the sacrament of baptism. By water and the Word God delivers us from sin and death and raises us to new life in Jesus Christ. We are united with all the baptized in the one body of Christ, anointed with the gift of the Holy Spirit, and joined in God's mission for the life of the world. (Holy Baptism, *Evangelical Lutheran Worship*, p. 227)

By now, you have probably picked up on certain themes repeated throughout this devotional book:

- You are not alone in your marriage, for Christ and the church are with you always.

- Your marriage is not just about yourselves but is an opportunity to live out your baptismal callings together.

Both themes are, at their core, tied to your baptisms. You are not alone because you share with the whole church on earth a baptism into the death and resurrection of Jesus Christ. By virtue of your baptisms you are joined in God's mission for the life of the world.

As months become years we hope and pray you will remember these two simple points. We also encourage you to return to this devotional from time to time. The words of scripture and the text of the marriage service will hold new meaning for you each time you read and meditate on them.

May God grant you many years to joyfully discover the wonders of one another and the blessings of married life together. Amen. Go in peace. Serve the Lord. Thanks be to God.

Appendix

Marriage Service—Evangelical Lutheran Worship

Introduction

Marriage is a gift of God, intended for the joy and mutual strength of those who enter it and for the well-being of the whole human family. God created us male and female and blessed humankind with the gifts of companionship, the capacity to love, and the care and nurture of children. Jesus affirmed the covenant of marriage and revealed God's own self-giving love on the cross. The Holy Spirit helps those who are united in marriage to be living signs of God's grace, love, and faithfulness.

Marriage is also a human estate, with vows publicly witnessed. The church in worship surrounds these promises with the gathering of God's people, the witness of the word of God, and prayers of blessing and intercession.

Pattern for Worship—Marriage

Gathering
The Holy Spirit gathers us in worship as we witness the marriage.

Entrance
Greeting
Declaration of Intention
Prayer of the Day

Gathered by the Holy Spirit and greeted in the name of the triune God, the assembly joins in worship. Those to be married state their intention; the assembly promises support. All are gathered into prayer.

Word
God speaks to us in scripture reading, preaching, and song.

Readings
Sermon
Hymn of the Day

Scripture readings, preaching, and song witness to the gift and vocation of marriage, bringing God's word of law and promise into this context of human life.

Marriage
As two become one by their promises, God blesses them.

Vows
Acclamation
Marriage Blessing
Prayers of Intercession
Lord's Prayer

The two pledge their love and faithfulness; the giving of rings is a symbol of this promise. The minister announces the marriage, and the assembly acclaims it. The prayers ask God's blessing upon this marriage and remember the needs of the whole world.

Meal
God sets out a marriage feast for all those joined to Christ.

Sending
God blesses us and sends us in mission to the world.

Peace
Blessing

Together with the newly married, we go out into the world with God's peace and blessing.

Marriage

Evangelical Lutheran Worship Leaders Edition

Gathering

Entrance

The assembly stands as the ministers and the wedding group enter. Music—hymn, song, psalm, instrumental music—may accompany the entrance.

Greeting

The presiding minister and the assembly greet each other.
The grace of our Lord Jesus Christ, the love of God,
and the communion of the Holy Spirit be with you all.
And also with you.

The minister may introduce the service with these or similar words.
Dear friends: We have come together in the presence of God to witness the marriage of <u>name</u> and <u>name,</u> to surround them with our prayers, and to share in their joy.

The scriptures teach us that the bond and covenant of marriage is a gift of God in which a man and a woman are joined as one, an image of the union of Christ and the church. As <u>name</u> and <u>name</u> make their promises to each other today, we remember that at Cana in Galilee our Lord Jesus Christ made the wedding feast a sign of God's reign of love.

Let us enter into this celebration confident that, through the Holy Spirit, Christ is present with us now also. We pray that this couple may fulfill God's purpose for the whole of their lives.

OR

The Lord God in goodness created us male and female, and by the gift of marriage founded human community in a joy that begins now and is brought to perfection in the life to come.

Because of sin, our age-old rebellion, the gladness of marriage can be overcast and the gift of a family can become a burden. But because God, who established marriage, continues still to bless it with abundant and ever-present support, we can be sustained in our weakness and have our joy restored.

Name and _name_ have come to make their marriage vows in the presence of God and of this assembly. The uniting of this man and this woman in heart, body, and mind is intended by God for their mutual joy, for the help and comfort they give one another in prosperity and adversity, and that their love may be a blessing to all whom they encounter.

Let us now witness their promises to each other and surround them with our prayers, giving thanks to God for the gift of marriage and asking God's blessing upon them, that they may be strengthened for their life together and nurtured in the love of God.

Declaration of Intention

Those who are declaring their intention to marry may be accompanied by their parents. The parents may place a hand on the shoulders of their children while responding to the question addressed to families.

The minister addresses the couple in these or similar words, asking each person in turn:
Name , will you have _name_ to be your _wife/husband,_ to live together in the covenant of marriage? Will you love _her/him,_ comfort _her/him,_ honor and keep _her/him,_ in sickness and in health, and, forsaking all others, be faithful to _her/him_ as long as you both shall live?
Response: I will.

OR

Name, will you receive _name_ as your _wife/husband_ and bind yourself to _her/him_ in the covenant of marriage? Will you promise to love and honor _her/him_ in true devotion, to rejoice with _her/him_ in times of gladness, to grieve with _her/him_ in times of sorrow, and to be faithful to _her/him_ as long as you both shall live?
Response: I will.

OR

Name , living in the promise of God, [joined to Christ in baptism,] will you give yourself to _name_ in love and faithfulness? Will you share your life with _her/him,_ in joy and in sorrow, in health and in sickness, for richer, for poorer, for better, for worse, and will you be faithful to _her/him_ as long as you both shall live?
Response: I will.

If pastorally advisable, the minister may address the families of the couple in these or similar words.
Will you, the families of _name_ and _name,_ give your love and blessing to this new family?
The families respond: **We will.**

The minister may address the assembly in these or similar words.

OR

Will all of you, by God's grace,
uphold and care for _name_ and _name_
in their life together?
We will.

Families, friends,
and all those gathered here with _name_ and _name,_
will you support and care for them,
sustain and pray for them in times of trouble,
give thanks with them in times of joy,
honor the bonds of their covenant,
and affirm the love of God reflected
in their life together?
We will.

Prayer of the Day

The presiding minister leads the prayer of the day.
Let us pray. *A brief silence is kept.*

OR

Gracious God,
you sent your Son Jesus Christ into the
world to reveal your love to all people.
Enrich _name_ and _name_ with every
good gift, that their life together
may show forth your love;
and grant that at the last
we may all celebrate with Christ
the marriage feast that has no end;
In the name of Jesus Christ our Lord.
Amen.

Eternal God, our creator and redeemer,
as you gladdened the wedding at Cana in Galilee
by the presence of your Son,
so bring your joy to this wedding
by his presence now.
Look in favor upon _name_ and _name_ and grant that
they, rejoicing in all your gifts,
may at length celebrate the unending marriage
feast with Christ our Lord,
who lives and reigns with you and the Holy Spirit,
one God, now and forever.
Amen.

Word

Readings

The assembly is seated. Two or three scripture readings are proclaimed. When the service includes communion, the last is a reading from the gospels. Responses may include a psalm in response to a reading from the Old Testament, a sung acclamation preceding the reading of the gospel, or other appropriate hymns, songs, and psalms.

Sermon

Silence for reflection follows.

Hymn of the Day

A hymn of the day may be sung.

Marriage

Vows

The presiding minister may address the couple in these or similar words.
Name and *name*, I invite you to declare your vows to one another.
The couple may join hands. Each promises faithfulness to the other in these or similar words.

OR

I take you, *name*,
to be my *wife/husband*
from this day forward,
to join with you
and share all that is to come,
and I promise to be faithful to you
until death parts us.

In the presence of God and this community,
I, *name*, take you, *name*,
to be my *wife/husband*;
to have and to hold from this day forward,
in joy and in sorrow, in plenty and in want,
in sickness and in health, to love and to cherish,
as long as we both shall live.
This is my solemn vow.

Giving of Rings

When rings are to be exchanged, the presiding minister may say this prayer.
Let us pray. We give you thanks, O God of grace, for your love and faithfulness to your people. May these rings be symbols of the promise *name* and *name* have made with each other; through Jesus Christ, our Savior and Lord.
Amen.

The couple may exchange rings with these or similar words.

<u>Name</u>, I give you this ring as a sign of my love and faithfulness.

OR

<u>Name</u>, I give you this ring as a symbol of my vow.
With all that I am, and all that I have, I honor you,
in the name of the Father, and of the Son, and of the Holy Spirit.

Acclamation

The presiding minister addresses the assembly. In places where the announcement of marriage is prescribed by law, that form should be used instead.

<u>Name</u> and <u>name</u>, by their promises before God and in the presence of this assembly, have joined themselves to one another as husband and wife. Those whom God has joined together let no one separate.
Amen. Thanks be to God.

The assembly may offer acclamation with applause. A sung acclamation, hymn, or other music may follow.

Other symbols of marriage may be given or used at this time.

Marriage Blessing

The couple may kneel. The presiding minister may extend a hand over the couple while praying for God's blessing in the following or similar words.

Most gracious God, we give you thanks for your tender love in sending Jesus Christ to come among us, to be born of a human mother, and to endure the cross for our sake, that we may have abundance of life.

By the power of your Holy Spirit pour out the abundance of your blessing on <u>name</u> and <u>name</u>. Defend them from every enemy. Lead them into all peace. Let your love be a seal upon their hearts, a mantle about their shoulders, and a crown upon their foreheads.

Bless them so that their lives together may bear witness to your love. Bless them in their work and in their companionship; in their sleeping and in their waking; in their joys and in their sorrows; in their life and in their death.

Finally, in your mercy, bring them to that table where your saints feast forever in your heavenly home, through Jesus Christ our Lord, who lives and reigns with you and the Holy Spirit, one God, now and forever.

Amen.

OR

The Lord God,
who created our first parents and established them in marriage,
establish and sustain you, that you may find delight in each other
and grow in holy love until your life's end.

Amen.

Parents or others may speak additional words of blessing and encouragement at this time.

Prayers of Intercession

The assembly stands. Prayers of intercession for the world and its needs may be prayed. These prayers, prepared or adapted for the particular occasion, may include the following or similar petitions. An assisting minister may lead the prayers.

I

Seeing how greatly God has loved us, let us pray for the whole world.

For the Christian community everywhere; for the life and ministry of the baptized, and for all servants of the gospel, that the church may be the risen body of Christ in the world. Gracious and faithful God,

hear our prayer.

For all who are joined by bonds of marriage, kinship, and friendship, and for communities everywhere; for the nations, for all those who govern, and for justice and peace throughout the world. Gracious and faithful God,

hear our prayer.

For those we love easily, and for those with whom we struggle, for those different from us and for those familiar to us, that we might be instruments of God's peace. Gracious and faithful God,

hear our prayer.

For those who suffer in any way, and those who are lonely, for the sick, the dying, and those who are bereaved, for those who are poor, hungry, homeless, or unemployed, for the victims of violence, hatred, and intolerance. Gracious and faithful God,
hear our prayer.

For all those who are joined to us in love; for our families, friends, and neighbors, for those separated from us by distance or discord,and giving thanks also for those who have gone before us (especially *name/s*). Gracious and faithful God,
hear our prayer.
Other intercessions may be added.

The presiding minister concludes the prayers.
Creator of all, you make us in your image and likeness and fill us with everlasting life. Hear the prayers of your people and grant to *name* and *name* grace to live in unity and joy all the days of their lives; through Jesus Christ, our Savior and Lord, to whom, with you and the Holy Spirit, be honor and praise forever.
Amen.

II
On this day of rejoicing, let us bless God for divine love made flesh in Jesus Christ.

We praise you, O God, for the joy that *name* and *name* have found in each other, and we pray that their love and faithfulness may reflectyour gracious love and enrich our common life. Gracious and faithful God,
hear our prayer.

Give them gentleness and patience, affection and understanding, readiness to trust one another, and, when they hurt each other, grace to acknowledge their fault and to give and receive forgiveness. Gracious and faithful God,
hear our prayer.

If pastorally advisable:
Give to *name* and *name* the gift and heritage of children
in accordance with your will; make their home a haven of peace.
OR
You have given *name* and *name* the gift and heritage of children;
make their home a haven of peace.

Gracious and faithful God,
hear our prayer.

Use us to support _name_ and _name_ in their lives together. Give us such a sense of your constant love that we may employ all our strength in a life of praise of you. Gracious and faithful God,
hear our prayer.

Strengthen and bless friends and family gathered here, even as we call to mind those who are absent from us. Console those who mourn the loss of loved ones, and be present with those for whom love is a stranger. Gracious and faithful God,
hear our prayer.

Look graciously on the world you have made and for which your Son gave his life. Strengthen marriages, families, and communities everywhere. Defend and guide all who suffer want or anxiety. Gracious and faithful God,
hear our prayer.

Other intercessions may be added.

We give thanks to you, merciful God, for those who have died (especially _name/s_). Strengthen us by the example of the saints, and bring us all to the marriage feast of the Lamb. Gracious and faithful God,
hear our prayer.

The presiding minister concludes the prayers.
Most gracious God, you have made us in your image and given us over to one another's care. Hear the prayers of your people, that unity may overcome division, hope vanquish despair, and joy conquer sorrow; through Jesus Christ our Lord.
Amen.

A service with communion continues with the peace. After the presiding minister greets the assembly, the couple may greet each other with the kiss of peace, and the assembly may greet one another in peace.

After the communion, the service concludes with this prayer and the blessing and sending.
Loving God, we thank you that you have fed us in this holy meal, united us with Christ, and given us a foretaste of the heavenly banquet. So strengthen us in your service that our daily lives may show our thanks, through Jesus Christ our Lord.
Amen.

A service without communion concludes as follows.

Lord's Prayer

The presiding minister may introduce the Lord's Prayer.

Gathered into one by the Holy Spirit, let us pray as Jesus taught us.

OR

Lord, remember us in your kingdom and teach us to pray.

OR

Our Father in heaven,	Our Father, who art in heaven,
hallowed be your name,	hallowed be thy name,
your kingdom come,	thy kingdom come,
your will be done,	thy will be done,
on earth as in heaven.	on earth as it is in heaven.
Give us today our daily bread.	Give us this day our daily bread;
Forgive us our sins	and forgive us our trespasses,
as we forgive those	as we forgive those
who sin against us.	who trespass against us;
Save us from the time of trial	and lead us not into temptation,
and deliver us from evil.	but deliver us from evil.
For the kingdom, the power,	For thine is the kingdom,
and the glory are yours,	and the power, and the glory,
now and forever. Amen.	forever and ever. Amen.

Sending

Peace

If it has not been included earlier in the service, the greeting of peace may be shared.

The peace of Christ be with you always.

And also with you.

The couple may greet one another with the kiss of peace. All present may greet one another with a gesture of peace, and may say Peace be with you *or similar words.*

Blessing

The presiding minister proclaims God's blessing in these or similar words.

OR

The blessed and holy Trinity
make you strong in faith and love,
defend you on every side,
and guide you in truth and peace,
now and forever.
Amen.

God Almighty
send you light and truth
to keep you all the days of your life.
The hand of God protect you;
the holy angels accompany you;
and the blessing of almighty God,
the Father, the ✠ Son, and the Holy Spirit,
be with you now and forever.
Amen.

Dismissal

An assisting minister may send the assembly forth in these or similar words.
Go in peace. Serve the Lord.
Thanks be to God.

A hymn may be sung or instrumental music played as the wedding group and the ministers depart.